GOLF

FACTS, FIGURES & FUN

*"Any book without a mistake in it has had
too much money spent on it"*

Sir William Collins, publisher

GOLF

Facts, Figures & Fun

Ed Harris

Golf
Facts, Figures & Fun

Published by
Facts, Figures & Fun, an imprint of
AAPPL Artists' and Photographers' Press Ltd.
Church Farm House, Wisley, Surrey GU23 6QL
info@ffnf.co.uk www.ffnf.co.uk
info@aappl.com www.aappl.com

Sales and Distribution
UK and export: Turnaround Publisher Services Ltd.
orders@turnaround-uk.com
USA and Canada: Sterling Publishing Inc.
sales@sterlingpub.com
Australia & New Zealand: Peribo Pty.
michael.coffey@peribo.com.au
South Africa: Trinity Books. trinity@iafrica.com

Seaside Golf by John Betjeman is reproduced
by kind permission of John Murray (Publishers)

A catalogue record for this book is available from the
British Library.

ISBN 13: 9781 904 332 657
ISBN 10: 1904 332 65X

Design (contents and cover): Malcolm Couch
mal.couch@blueyonder.co.uk

Printed in China by Imago Publishing
info@imago.co.uk

CONTENTS

INTRODUCTION
GOLF: SPORT, SNOBBERY OR OBSESSION?

This is not a long book and it deals with an immense subject. Many books and articles have been written about golf, and any comprehensive survey of all aspects of the sport would be an enormous volume.

The contents of this book are therefore highly selective and this is clearly a personal selection. I have tried to present a mixture of facts, statistics, opinion and humour which I hope most of all that readers will find to be interesting and even occasionally useful.

THE NAME

"Golf is an infuriating game that brings out the worst in people. Why was it called golf? Because all the other four letter words were taken."

There are those who believe that the word golf stands for "Gentlemen Only, Ladies Forbidden", and whereas there may be much truth in this (see later), the reality is more prosaic.

One theory is that the word originates from the Scottish word "goff" which means to strike, as in to cuff someone. The main body of opinion however is that the original term is the Dutch "kolf" meaning club, in the sense of a stick or cudgel. The German word "kolbe", meaning club, may also be linked.

··············ORIGINS OF GOLF··············

There are numerous claims from various parts of the world to be the ancient birthplace of the game. The most common opinion of course, is that the game originated in Scotland. There are however two other plausible candidates for originating golf.

The Egyptian Pharaoh Tuthmosis III (18th dynasty, BC 1490-1436) is recorded as playing a game where he hit balls with a wooden club. The balls were placed by priests and collected by slaves. This at least can be put forward as the very first documented driving range.

There is a much stronger case, arising from the name golf, that the game started in the Netherlands. This is further supported by trade documents from the 16th century which appear to show that balls being used in Scotland were imported from the Netherlands.

We must however give the credit to the Scots for the invention of the game in the 15th century. Clearly prior to that time there existed numerous games where sticks were used to hits balls, but the essential element of golf is that the ball is hit (finally) into a hole in the ground. There is no plausible evidence that this originated anywhere other than Scotland.

*"Golf was just what the Scottish character had been seeking
for centuries namely a method of self-torture, disguised as a
game, which would entrap irreligious youths into principles
of what was to become known first as Calvinism and then as
golf. The main tenets of this faith are that life is grim and
uncomfortable and that human vanity cannot prevail.
The golfer's credo is that men should expect very little here
below and strive to gain it."*
Alistair Cooke.

HISTORY OF GOLF

Golf, basically as we know it today, began in Scotland
sometime in the early 15th century.

The first record of golf is an edict issued by King James
II of Scotland in 1457 banning the game (and soccer).
His problem was that his subjects were neglecting their
archery skills and practice. Most importantly the English
were developing their archery. Similar edicts were issued
by James III in 1471 and James IV in 1491.

By 1502 the edicts banning golf had been rescinded,
and the first recorded golf course began in Perth. Other
recorded courses were Carnoustie (1527), Montrose
(1562), Musselburgh (1567) and St Andrews (1574).
During these years, and during the period of the bans,
golf was also played on various areas of open land.

Golf in Scotland during this early period was the
subject of vocal criticism from the Kirk, particularly
playing on Sundays. In 1567, Mary Queen of Scots was
the subject of severe criticism from the Calvinist John
Knox and the Kirk for playing golf only two days after the
death of her husband Darnley. The fact that she had
arranged his murder may have added to the volume of the
criticism.

This record of Mary playing golf indicates that the game had become popular amongst royalty and the aristocracy. Mary's son James VI is recorded as playing golf for large bets, and on becoming James I of England he brought the game south of the border. (See later).

As well as golf courses, golf clubs began to emerge in Scotland. The early recorded ones are the Royal Burgess Golf Society (1735), Honourable Company of Edinburgh Golfers (1744), and the Royal & Ancient Golf Club of St Andrews, known as the R&A (1754). Together with the aristocratic interest in golf, the creation of these clubs signals the beginning of a social element and snobbery in the game.

Golf in England began with the accession of James I. He played golf on Blackheath Common. This is the earliest record of golf outside Scotland.

The oldest club in England is Royal Blackheath. Golf is recorded being played on Blackheath Common in 1608. The club was founded in 1745. The oldest golf club in England playing on its original course is Westward Ho! (1864). (Now Royal North Devon).

The first recorded golf club outside Great Britain is the Dum Dum Club in Calcutta, India (1829). (Later Royal Calcutta).

Golf appeared in Australia in 1871 in Adelaide, however Royal Melbourne claims to be the oldest club. Claims that the Bothwell Golf Club opened in Tasmania in 1830 cannot be substantiated.

Royal Montreal is the oldest club in North America (1873). In USA although there are records of golf being played earlier in West Virginia, it is generally accepted that the oldest club is St Andrews in Ardley-on-Hudson, NY.

In Continental Europe, golf was played in the Iberian Peninsula by officers of Wellington's army during the Peninsular War. The first club was in Pau, France, founded by British expatriates in 1856.

In Japan, where golf is immensely popular, the game was introduced in Kobe in 1901 by an English merchant, Arthur Hesketh Groom. He also introduced cricket which did not apparently appeal to the Japanese character. Many of the early players were expatriates. Inoe Shin in 1918 is the first recorded Japanese winner of a tournament.

The farthest expansion, so far, of golf is the Moon. In 1971 astronaut Alan Shepherd hit a ball with a 6 iron and it disappeared out of sight!

·······DEVELOPMENT OF THE GAME·······

Golf was originally played in Scotland in a variety of open locations. This was one of two forms of the game becoming known as "short" golf. It was played by the general populace around churchyards and village greens often hitting balls at targets rather than holes. It was this game that so annoyed the government and the Kirk. In Kelso in 1632, the death of an apparently innocent bystander is recorded. The modern game developed from "links" golf which was generally played by aristocracy and wealthier individuals on waste land, particularly land close to the sea. It may be that links golf was played in remote locations to circumvent the royal edicts banning the game. From the early 17th century, only the links type of golf developed.

Courses, both in Scotland and elsewhere, had varied numbers of holes in this early period. The present 18 hole standard emerged in the late 19th century.

·················· COMPETITIONS ··················

Competitions amongst amateur players date from the time of the beginnings of the game. James I&VI is recorded as playing against Earl Bothwell for sizeable bets. The R&A began in 1754 with a "Silver Cup", the winner becoming Captain for the year. In 1806 the Club started a "Gold Medal" competition. William IV became patron of the Club in 1834 and presented the "Royal Medal" in 1836.

The first professional competition was the Open Championship which was started by Prestwick Golf Club in 1860. The R&A took over the running of the Open in 1872.

The first Amateur Championship was inaugurated by Royal Liverpool Golf Club in 1885.

The first major competition outside UK was the US Open in 1895.

EQUIPMENT AND DRESS

"The game consists of putting little balls into little holes with instruments very ill-adapted for the purpose."
Winston Churchill.

There is some doubt if Churchill ever said this but it is the kind of thing he would have said. The comment was probably quite accurate at the time it was made. Today however the quality and variety of golf equipment is considerable. Much of the focus of the present day regulators is on limiting the performance of equipment so as to fit within the limitations of existing golf courses.

The makeup of the golf ball has changed considerably over the years. From the 15th century up to the 1860s, the balls were leather covers stuffed with feathers, known as "featheries". The ball was manufactured with wet leather and feathers which hardened as they dried.

From about 1860 the "gutty" came into use. The gutty was a solid ball made from gutta percha, a hard rubbery substance from India. These balls, as they were used, acquired nicks and cuts from being hit. It was noticed that these balls then flew further than the undamaged ones. This eventually led to the development of the dimple type of ball which we have today. The invention of

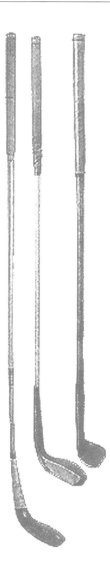

the gutty is sometimes attributed to a Reverend R. Patterson, who was sent a parcel from India, the contents of which were wrapped in gutta percha. The parcel was placed close to a fire and Dr Patterson noticed that it had become quite malleable, so he moulded it into a golf ball. This story loses much credibility as no one has ever been able to identify the existence of this individual.

The next major ball development was invented by Coburn Haskell, a Chicago dentist, who in the 1890s developed the "wound" ball, a technique still in use today for some three piece balls. This was improved by James Foulis, the US Open Champion in 1896, who developed the dimpled casing which caused the ball to fly a much greater distance. Some gutties were also given the dimpled cover, however they rapidly fell out of use after an American, Sandy Herd, beat Harry Vardon in the Open at Hoylake in 1902.

Today, golf balls are either two piece or three piece. Two piece balls have a solid rubber core usually with a cover made from Surlyn, a synthetic substance highly resistant to cuts. Professionals generally prefer three  piece balls with a liquid centre wound with elastic and a balata cover. In addition to the regular circle dimple pattern on covers, some balls are DDH (dodecahedron patterned). Today balls must be a minimum of 1.68 inches in diameter and weigh not more than 1.62 ounces. There is no maximum size specified and balls may be of any colour.

Currently much attention is given by the regulators to limiting the playing characteristics of golf balls. Today technology is readily available to manufacture balls which will travel tremendous distances, far in excess of traditional balls. The R&A tests balls at St Andrews with a machine that hits them on a consistent basis. The initial velocity must not exceed 250 feet per second at an ambient temperature of 23C and the balls must not travel more than 256 metres (+/- 6%). Up to 2000 the USGA had a machine known as "Iron Byron", named after Byron Nelson (see later) who was reputed to have the perfect and consistent swing.

Originally clubs had shafts made from a variety of harder woods, but eventually hickory shafts became the norm. Clubs had names like cleek, niblick, mashie, blaster, and rutting iron. Steel shafts were invented in 1913 by Sidney Saunders, who was a manager in a Birmingham steel mill.

The R&A promptly banned them until the Prince of Wales used a set in 1929, and the ban was then lifted. By this time hickory was becoming scarce, and some alternative was needed. Throughout the 20th century, clubs have developed considerably, mainly in terms of new materials. Graphite shafts add considerably to performance (for less skilled players) and metals such as titanium have enabled clubheads to increase in size without increases in weight. As is the case with golf balls, the regulators are working incessantly to keep technical improvements within limits.

The present system of numbered clubs with differing angles of elevation developed gradually during the 20th century. Perhaps the most important individual contribution came from Gene Sarazen who invented the sand iron. Grooves on the club face have been and continue to be a headache for the regulators. The first use of grooved clubs was by Tom Kidd whose club faces were described as being "suitable for grating nutmeg". He won the first Open held at St Andrews in 1873 with these clubs. In the 1920s, the USGA introduced the "Anderson Formula" to regulate grooving. This lasted until the 1960s when Ping introduced square section grooves which the USGA then banned. After some years of vicious litigation, Ping eventually withdrew these clubs in the late 1990s.

The Ping company was founded by Karl Solheim, a Norwegian born American aircraft engineer. In 1959 Solheim thought that he could improve the design of the traditional putter. He developed the "heel and toe weighted" offset putter, which has become the most popular club of all time. Ping presents a gold plated replica putter to every winner of a major event using the Ping putter. They have presented over 2000 since 1967.

Over the years, golf clothing has developed considerably. During the 19th century players generally played in suits, often with breeches, wearing heavy hobnailed shoes or boots. Today fashions are much more relaxed and comfortable. Much of the development of specialized golf clothing can be attributed to Ernie Sabayrac, originally a caddie from Houston, Texas. Sabayrac introduced the first spiked golf shoes and later specialized golf clothes with badges and logos. When he died in 1997, he was a very rich man.

HANDICAP SYSTEM AND SCORING

Prior to the very late 19th century, golf was played simply on the basis of using the least number of shots to sink the ball without reference to any standard. In 1890 Hugh Rotherham, secretary of Coventry Golf Club developed the idea of standardising the number of shots at each hole that a good golfer should take. He called this the "ground score". The idea was then taken up by Dr Browne, the secretary of the Great Yarmouth Golf Club, and the system was put into use there. It was at Great Yarmouth that the word "Bogey" came to be used in referring to the ground score, and for some time thereafter the word Bogey was used throughout Great Britain to signify the ground score. The word probably comes from Bogey Man (devil or goblin), and this phrase was in vogue at the time due to a popular music hall song "Here comes the Bogey Man". Golfers in those days considered that they were playing against Mr Bogey in attempting to equal the ground score. This was altered at the United Services Club at Gosport where all the members held military ranks and could not be addressed as Mister. At this club Mr Bogey became Colonel Bogey, later the title of a famous march by Kenneth Alford with unofficial words referring to Adolf Hitler's anatomy.

At a later date, Bogey came to be used as the term for one above Par.

The word "Par" derives from the London Stock Exchange where it denoted a stock price equal to the face value of the particular stock. Its use in golf started at Prestwick in Scotland in 1870 where it was used for the Open Championship. However throughout most of Great Britain the Bogey terminology continued to be used.

It was in the USA that a formal rating system began to develop. The US Women's Golf Association started the process in 1893, and had developed a national handicapping system by 1900 which included Par scores for many courses. The USGA quickly followed suit and in 1911 issued distances to be used for determining Par scores. These distances still apply today.

Up to 225 yards	Par 3
225 to 425 yards	Par 4
426 to 600 yards	Par 5
Over 600 yards	Par 6

During the early 20th century scores were declining so fast that many professional players were easily undercutting courses using the British Bogey system, and Americans began using Bogey to describe a score of one over Par. One deficiency of the British system was that Bogey was set by each individual club generally without reference to any national standard. It was not until 1925 that Standard Scratch Scores (SSS) were assigned to British and Irish courses, when the Golf Unions Joint Advisory Committee was formed.

The term Birdie, meaning one under Par, originates in the USA. In the 19th century the term "bird" was used as a slang word for something good or excellent. Reputedly the term Birdie was originated in about 1903 by two brothers Abe and William Smith who played at Atlantic City Country Club.

Eagle, meaning two under Par, derives from Birdie, being just a bigger bird and the US national symbol. Likewise an Albatross (three under Par) is an even bigger bird. Albatross is a quite recent term of unknown origin. It was generally known as a Double Eagle and Gene Sarazen, who scored one in the 1935 Masters, referred to his shot as a Dodo.

Basically, the rating and handicap systems and the terminology used today originated in the United States.

SUPERVISORY BODIES

The game of golf is administered by the R&A and the United States Golf Association. The USGA is responsible for North America and Mexico. The R&A is responsible for the rest of the world. The Rules of Golf are jointly agreed by the R&A and USGA and are reviewed jointly every four years.

The Society of St Andrews Golfers was founded May 14th 1754 when 22 noblemen and gentlemen of Fife

played for a silver cup. The winner became Captain for the subsequent year. In 1834 the name was changed to "The Royal and Ancient Golf Club of St Andrews" and King William IV became patron.

The R&A set up its "Rules of Golf" committee in 1897 and published the "Rules of Golf". Rules pertaining to clubs were issued in 1909 and rules about golf balls followed in 1920.

In that same year, 1920, the first conference was held with the USGA about rules. As a result of this meeting a uniform specification for the ball was agreed. This agreement was short-lived as the USGA increased the size of its ball in 1928 and increased the weight in 1932. The R&A changed to the American ball specification in 1988 thereby creating international uniformity.

In 1951, a conference between the R&A and USGA led to the issue of the 1952 Rules of Golf. Revisions were issued in 1954 and 1956, and subsequently every four years.

The R&A is also responsible for running the Open Championship and the Amateur Championship (both since 1920).

The USGA was set up in 1894 to administer the game in USA. It is located in Far Hills, NJ. As well as setting rules for golf it is responsible for running the national championships.

In addition to the R&A and USGA, most countries where golf is played have their own national associations who administer the game locally.

"Caddy, do you think it's a sin to play
golf on a Sunday?"
"The way you play, sir, it's a crime
any day of the week."

Major Championships

There are currently four "Major" annual golf championships, three in USA and one in Great Britain. They are:-

The Open (1860)
The US Open (1895)
The US PGA (1916)
The Masters (1934)

Five players have won all four Majors. They are:-

Gene Sarazen
Ben Hogan
Jack Nicklaus
Gary Player
Tiger Woods

No player has achieved the "Grand Slam" of winning all four events in the same year. Tiger Woods came closest to this in 2000, when he won the Open, the US Open, and the PGA.

Jack Nicklaus holds the record for the most Major wins with a total of 18.

THE OPEN CHAMPIONSHIP

*"Some weeks Nick (Faldo) likes to use Fanny,
other weeks he prefers to do it by himself."*
Ken Brown, BBC commentator,
at the 1997 Open Championship.

The Open is the oldest professional event in golf and the oldest of the Majors. The R&A initiated a "Grand National Tournament" in 1857 played by teams representing a number of clubs. This was modified to an individual tournament in 1858 played by "gentlemen players, members of any established golf club". It was played again in 1859. Today qualification for the Open is restricted to the top 50 in world rankings, the top 20 on the PGA tour, previous Open champions, any winner of a Major in the previous five years, and the top ten from the previous Open. In addition twelve places are reserved for "Local Qualifiers". It is played in July each year and is the third in sequence of the four Majors.

In 1860 at Prestwick Golf Club Lord Eglington thought it would be interesting to organize a tournament for caddies. It was considered a great success and renamed the Open Championship. In 1872 the R&A and Muirfield joined Prestwick in organizing the Open. Royal Liverpool, Royal St Georges, and Royal Cinque Ports joined later. In 1920 the R&A took sole responsibility.

From 1860 to 1870, the winner received the Championship Belt. After winning four consecutive times, Young Tom Morris kept the belt in 1870 and the present trophy, the Claret Jug was presented. The Jug was held for the longest period by Dick Burton, a club professional from Combe Hill, Surrey, who won it in 1939 and kept it until the next event in 1946, due of course to the war interval.

The early winners were Scottish professionals until the Englishman John Ball won in 1890. Ball was also the first amateur winner. English players then became more prominent in the winners' list and we enter into the era of J H Taylor and Harry Vardon. The first non-British winner was Arnaud Massy of France, to this day the only French winner. The American Jock Hutchison (who was born in Scotland) won in 1921 and the first American-born winner was Walter Hagen in 1922. Hagen won four times in the 1920s, and Bobby Jones, the great US amateur, won three times in 1926, 1927, and 1930. Prior to 1939 the Open title went outside the UK only thirteen times.

Fred Daly of Northern Ireland, who won in 1947, is the only Irish winner. The 1950s and early 1960s showed a strong colonial performance with Peter Thomson winning five times and Bobby Locke winning four times. American players dominated in the 1970s, Tom Watson winning five times and Jack Nicklaus three times. From the middle 1980s, the title was held by a worldwide selection of players, and Americans have won six of the seven championships since the millennium.

The Open moves around a number of links courses in Scotland and England. The courses which have been used most often are:-

St Andrews	27	Troon	8
Prestwick	24	Musselburgh	6
Muirfield	15	Carnoustie	6
Sandwich	13	Turnberry	3
Hoylake	11	Deal	2
Lytham	10	Portrush	1
Birkdale	8		

At the present time, there are nine courses in the rota. They are:-

> St Andrews
> Muirfield
> Royal St Georges
> Royal Liverpool
> Royal Troon
> Royal Lytham and St Annes
> Carnoustie
> Royal Birkdale
> Turnberry

The record for the most Open wins belongs to Harry Vardon with six wins between 1896 and 1914. Four players have won five titles. James Braid (1901-1910), J H Taylor (1894-1913), Peter Thomson (1954-1965), and Tom Watson (1975-1983).

The oldest winner was Old Tom Morris in 1867 at the age of 46. The following year 1868 his son Young Tom Morris became the youngest winner, age 17.

The Open is the only one of the four Majors to have been

won by fathers and sons. In addition to the Morrises, Willie Park Snr and Willie Park Jnr won the event.

OTHER RECORDS

Last amateur winner - Bobby Jones (1930)
Most amateur victories
Bobby Jones 3 (1926, 1927, 1930)
Biggest margin of victory
Old Tom Morris 13 strokes (1862)
Lowest winning aggregate
Greg Norman 267 Royal St Georges (1993)
Most successive victories
Young Tom Morris 4 (1868-1872)
Most rounds under par - Jack Nicklaus 61
Most aggregates under par - Jack Nicklaus 14
Most appearances - Gary Player 46
Most appearances without winning - Dai Rees 29
Most appearances before first victory - Nick Price 16
Most appearances on final day - Jack Nicklaus 32

WINNERS OF THE OPEN CHAMPIONSHIP

2006 Tiger Woods (US)	1998 Mark O'Meara (US)
2005 Tiger Woods (US)	1997 Justin Leonard (US)
2004 Todd Hamilton (US)	1996 Tom Lehman (US)
2003 Ben Curtis (US)	1995 John Daly (US)
2002 Ernie Els (SA)	1994 Nick Price (Zim)
2001 David Duval (US)	1993 Greg Norman (Aus)
2000 Tiger Woods (US)	1992 Nick Faldo (Eng)
1999 Paul Lawrie (Scot)	1991 Ian Baker-Finch (Aus)

1990 Nick Faldo (Eng)

1989 Mark Calcavecchia (US)

1988 Seve Ballesteros (Sp)

1987 Nick Faldo (Eng)

1986 Greg Norman (Aus)

1985 Sandy Lyle (Sco)

1984 Seve Ballesteros (Sp)

1983 Tom Watson (US)

1982 Tom Watson (US)

1981 Bill Rogers (US)

1980 Tom Watson (US)

1979 Seve Ballesteros (Sp)

1978 Jack Nicklaus (US)

1977 Tom Watson (US)

1976 Johnny Miller (US)

1975 Tom Watson (US)

1974 Gary Player (SA)

1973 Tom Weiskopf (US)

1972 Lee Trevino (US)

1971 Lee Trevino (US)

1970 Jack Nicklaus (US)

1969 Tony Jacklin (Eng)

1968 Gary Player (SA)

1967 Roberto DeVicenzo (Arg)

1966 Jack Nicklaus (US)

1965 Peter Thomson (Aus)

1964 Tony Lema (US)

1963 Bob Charles NZ

1962 Arnold Palmer (US)

1961 Arnold Palmer (US)

1960 Kel Nagle (NZ)

1959 Gary Player (SA)

1958 Peter Thomson (Aus)

1957 Bobby Locke (SA)

1956 Peter Thomson (Aus)

1955 Peter Thomson (Aus)

1954 Peter Thomson (Aus)

1953 Ben Hogan (US)

1952 Bobby Locke (SA)

1951 Max Faulkner (Eng)

1950 Bobby Locke (SA)

1949 Bobby Locke (SA)

1948 Henry Cotton (Eng)

1947 Fred Daly (NI)

1946 Sam Snead (US)

1940/45 *Second World War*

1939 Richard Burton (Eng)

1938 Reg Whitcombe (Eng)

1937 Henry Cotton (Eng)

1936 Alf Padgham (Eng)

1935 Alf Perry (Eng)

1934 Henry Cotton (Eng)

1933 Denny Shute (US)

1932 Gene Sarazen (US)

1931 Tommy Armour (US)

1930 Bobby Jones (am) (US)

1929 Walter Hagen (US)

1928 Walter Hagen (US)

1927 Bobby Jones (am) (US)

1926 Bobby Jones (am) (US)

1925 Jim Barnes (US)

1924 Walter Hagen (US)

1923 Arthur Havers (Eng)
1922 Walter Hagen (US)
1921 Jock Hutchison (US)
1920 George Duncan (Sco)
1915/19 *First World War*
1914 Harry Vardon (Eng)
1913 J H Taylor (Eng)
1912 Edward Ray (Eng)
1911 Harry Vardon (Eng)
1910 James Braid (Sco)
1909 J H Taylor (Eng)
1908 James Braid (Sco)
1907 Arnaud Massy (Fra)
1906 James Braid (Sco)
1905 James Braid (Sco)
1904 Jack White (Sco)
1903 Harry Vardon (Eng)
1902 Alexander Herd (Sco)
1901 James Braid (Sco)
1900 J H Taylor (Eng)
1899 Harry Vardon (Eng)
1898 Harry Vardon (Eng)
1897 Harold Hilton (am) (Eng)
1896 Harry Vardon (Eng)
1895 J H Taylor (Eng)
1894 J H Taylor (Eng)
1893 William Auchterlonie (Sco)
1892 Harold Hilton (am) (Eng)
1891 Hugh Kirkaldy (Sco)
1890 John Ball Jnr (am) (Eng)
1889 Willie Park Jnr (Sco)

1888 Jack Burns (Sco)
1887 Willie Park Jnr (Sco)
1886 David Brown (Sco)
1885 Bob Martin (Sco)
1884 Jack Simpson (Sco)
1883 Willie Fernie (Sco)
1882 Bob Ferguson (Sco)
1881 Bob Ferguson (Sco)
1880 Bob Ferguson (Sco)
1879 Jamie Anderson (Sco)
1878 Jamie Anderson (Sco)
1877 Jamie Anderson (Sco)
1876 Bob Martin (Sco)
1875 Willie Park Snr (Sco)
1874 Mungo Park (Sco)
1873 Tom Kidd (Sco)
1872 Tom Morris Jnr (Sco)
1871 *Not Played*
1870 Tom Morris Jnr (Sco)
1869 Tom Morris Jnr (Sco)
1868 Tom Morris Jnr (Sco)
1867 Tom Morris Snr (Sco)
1866 Willie Park Snr (Sco)
1865 Andrew Strath (Sco)
1864 Tom Morris Snr (Sco)
1863 Willie Park Snr (Sco)
1862 Tom Morris Snr (Sco)
1861 Tom Morris Snr (Sco)
1860 Willie Park Snr (Sco)

UNITED STATES OPEN

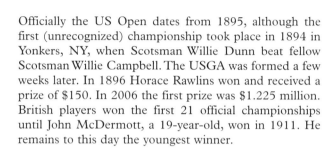

Officially the US Open dates from 1895, although the first (unrecognized) championship took place in 1894 in Yonkers, NY, when Scotsman Willie Dunn beat fellow Scotsman Willie Campbell. The USGA was formed a few weeks later. In 1896 Horace Rawlins won and received a prize of $150. In 2006 the first prize was $1.225 million. British players won the first 21 official championships until John McDermott, a 19-year-old, won in 1911. He remains to this day the youngest winner.

Four players have won the US Open four times.
Willie Anderson (1901,1903,1904,1905),
Bobby Jones (1923,1926,1929,1930),
Ben Hogan (1948,1950,1951,1953), and
Jack Nicklaus (1962,1967,1972,1980).
Willie Anderson holds the record of three consecutive wins. There have been eight amateur wins, four by Bobby Jones. The most recent amateur winner was Johnny Goodman in 1933.

Typically only about half of the field is exempt from qualifying, the smallest proportion in the Majors. Qualifying tournaments take place in USA, Japan, and Europe. The US Open is the second Major each year occurring in June.

OTHER RECORDS

Oldest winner: Hale Irwin (1990) 45 years
Youngest winner: John Mcdermott (1911) 19 years
Biggest winning margin: Tiger Woods (2000) 15 strokes
(*biggest margin in any Major*)
Lowest Aggregates: 272
Jack Nicklaus (1980) Baltusrol
Lee Janzen (1993) Baltusrol
Tiger Woods (2000) Pebble Beach
Jim Furyk (2003) Olympia Fields

WINNERS OF THE US OPEN.

2006 Geoff Ogilvy (Aus)	1978 Andy North (US)
2005 Michael Campbell (NZ)	1977 Hubert Green (US)
2004 Retief Goosen (SA)	1976 Jerry Pate (US)
2003 Jim Furyk (US)	1975 Lou Graham (US)
2002 Tiger Woods (US)	1974 Hale Irwin (US)
2001 Retief Goosen SA	1973 Johnny Miller (US)
2000 Tiger Woods (US)	1974 Jack Nicklaus (US)
1999 Payne Stewart (US)	1973 Johnny Miller (US)
1998 Lee Janzen (US)	1972 Jack Nicklaus (US)
1997 Ernie Els (SA)	1971 Lee Trevino (US)
1996 Steve Jones (US)	1970 Tony Jacklin (Eng)
1995 Corey Pavin (US)	1969 Orville Moody (US)
1994 Ernie Els (SA)	1968 Lee Trevino (US)
1993 Lee Janzen (US)	1967 Jack Nicklaus (US)
1992 Tom Kite (US)	1966 Billy Casper (US)
1991 Payne Stewart (US)	1965 Gary Player (SA)
1990 Hale Irwin (US)	1964 Ken Venturi (US)
1989 Curtis Strange (US)	1963 Julius Boros (US)
1988 Curtis Strange (US)	1962 Jack Nicklaus (US)
1987 Scott Simpson (US)	1961 Gene Littler (US)
1986 Ray Floyd (US)	1960 Arnold Palmer (US)
1985 Andy North (US)	1959 Billy Casper (US)
1984 Fuzzy Zoeller (US)	1958 Tommy Bolt (US)
1983 Larry Nelson (US)	1957 Dick Mayer (US)
1982 Tom Watson (US)	1956 Cary Middlecoff (US)
1981 David Graham (Aus)	1955 Jack Fleck (US)
1980 Jack Nicklaus (US)	1954 Ed Furgol (US)
1979 Hale Irwin (US)	1953 Ben Hogan (US)

1952 Julius Boros (US)
1951 Ben Hogan (US)
1950 Ben Hogan (US)
1949 Cary Middlecoff (US)
1948 Ben Hogan (US)
1947 Lew Worsham (US)
1946 Lloyd Mangrum (US)
1940/45 *Second World War*
1941 Craig Wood (US)
1940 Lawson Little (US)
1939 Byron Nelson (US)
1938 Ralph Guldahl (US)
1937 Ralph Guldahl (US)
1936 Tony Manero (US)
1935 Sam Parks Jnr (US)
1934 Olin Dutra (US)
1933 Johnny Goodman
   (am) (US)
1932 Gene Sarazen (US)
1931 Billy Burke (US)
1930 Bobby Jones (am) (US)
1929 Bobby Jones (am) (US)
1928 Johnny Farrell (US)
1927 Tommy Armour (US)
1926 Bobby Jones (am) (US)
1925 W MacFarlane (Sco)
1924 Cyril Walker (Eng)
1923 Bobby Jones (am) (US)
1922 Gene Sarazen (US)

1921 James M Barnes (US)
1920 Edward Ray (Eng)
1919 Walter Hagen (US)
1917/18 *First World War*
1916 Charles Evans Jnr
   (am) (US)
1915 Jerome Travers (am) (US)
1914 Walter Hagen (US)
1913 Francis Ouimet (am) (US)
1912 John McDermott (US)
1911 John McDermott (US)
1910 Alex Smith (Sco)
1909 George Sargent (Eng)
1908 Fred McLeod (Sco)
1907 Alex Ross (Sco)
1906 Alex Smith (Sco)
1905 Willie Anderson (Sco)
1904 Willie Anderson (Sco)
1903 Willie Anderson (Sco)
1902 Laurie Auchterlonie
   (Sco)
1901 Willie Anderson (Sco)
1900 Harry Vardon (Eng)
1899 Willie Smith (Sco)
1898 Fred Herd (Sco)
1897 Joe Lloyd (Eng)
1896 James Foulis (Sco)
1895 Horace Rawlins (Eng)

THE MASTERS

"Ballesteros felt much better today after a 69."
Steve Ryder, BBC commentator at the Masters.

The Masters is an invitational event founded by Bobby Jones and Clifford Roberts in 1934. Bobby Jones himself was not in favour of calling it "The Masters" and until 1939 it was called the "Augusta National Invitation Tournament". It is the only Major always played on the same course at Augusta National Golf Club, Georgia. The course was designed by Jones and Alister MacKensie and is regarded as being very difficult, at the same time being one of the most attractive courses anywhere. It is the first Major each year, taking place in early April.

There were no non-American winners until Gary Player won in 1961. The greatest numbers of wins were scored by Jack Nicklaus (1963,1965,1966,1972,1975,1986) followed by Arnold Palmer (1958,1960,1962,1964) and Tiger Woods (1997,2001,2002,2005) with four wins each.

Gene Sarazen in the 1935 Masters played one of the most momentous shots ever seen in golf. He holed a shot from the fairway on the par 5 15th hole to score a double eagle (albatross). He tied for the title and won the subsequent playoff.

The Masters involves certain attributes which do not occur in the other Majors. Augusta National is a private club which still does not admit female members despite protests from activists. Until recent times, no non-white members or players were admitted. Lee Elder became the first black American to play in the event in 1975. Until 1983, players were obliged to use a club caddie. Players may now use their regular caddies but the caddies must still wear the Augusta uniform of white jumpsuit and green cap.

In addition to cash and silverware, the winner receives a green club blazer. Traditionally this is presented by the previous year's winner.

The youngest winner is Tiger Woods in 1997 aged 21 years. The oldest winner is Jack Nicklaus in 1986 at 46 years.

OTHER RECORDS

Biggest winning margin – Tiger Woods 12 strokes (1997)
Most appearances – Arnold Palmer 50
Most cuts made – Jack Nicklaus 37

WINNERS OF THE MASTERS

2006 Phil Mickelson (US)	1999 Jose Maria Olazabal (Sp)
2005 Tiger Woods (US)	1998 Mark O'Meara (US)
2004 Phil Mickelson (US)	1997 Tiger Woods (US)
2003 Mike Weir (Can)	1996 Nick Faldo (Eng)
2002 Tiger Woods (US)	1995 Ben Crenshaw (US)
2001 Tiger Woods (US)	1994 Jose Maria Olazabal (Sp)
2000 Vijay Singh (Fiji)	1993 Bernhard Langer (Ger)

1992 Fred Couples (US)
1991 Ian Woosnam (Wales)
1990 Nick Faldo (Eng)
1989 Nick Faldo (Eng)
1988 Sandy Lyle (Sco)
1987 Larry Mize (US)
1986 Jack Nicklaus (US)
1985 Bernhard Langer (Ger)
1984 Ben Crenshaw (US)
1983 Seve Ballesteros (Sp)
1982 Craig Stadler (US)
1981 Tom Watson (US)
1980 Seve Ballesteros (Sp)
1979 Fuzzy Zoeller (US)
1978 Gary Player (SA)
1977 Tom Watson (US)
1976 Ray Floyd (US)
1975 Jack Nicklaus (US)
1974 Gary Player (SA)
1973 Tommy Aaron (US)
1972 Jack Nicklaus (US)
1971 Charles Coody (US)
1970 Billy Casper (US)
1969 George Archer (US)
1968 Bob Goalby (US)
1967 Gay Brewer (US)
1966 Jack Nicklaus (US)
1965 Jack Nicklaus (US)
1964 Arnold Palmer (US)

1963 Jack Nicklaus (US)
1962 Arnold Palmer (US)
1961 Gary Player (SA)
1960 Arnold Palmer (US)
1959 Art Wall (US)
1958 Arnold Palmer (US)
1957 Doug Ford (US)
1956 Jack Burke Jnr (US)
1955 Cary Middlecoff (US)
1954 Sam Snead (US)
1953 Ben Hogan (US)
1952 Sam Snead (US)
1951 Ben Hogan (US)
1950 Jimmy Demaret (US)
1949 Sam Snead (US)
1948 Claude Harmon (US)
1947 Jimmy Demaret (US)
1946 Herman Keiser (US)
1943/45 *Second World War*
1942 Byron Nelson (US)
1941 Craig Wood (US)
1940 Jimmy Demaret (US)
1939 Ralph Guldahl (US)
1938 Henry Picard (US)
1937 Byron Nelson (US)
1936 Horton Smith (US)
1935 Gene Sarazen (US)
1934 Horton Smith (US)

US PGA

"One of the reasons Arnie (Arnold Palmer) is playing so well is that, before each tee shot, his wife takes out his balls and kisses them.....Oh my God! What have I just said?"
American TV commentator at the
1960 US PGA Championship.

The US PGA Championship was founded in 1916 to mark the foundation of the Professional Golfers Association of America. The first event was held at Bronxville, NY, and was won by Jim Barnes who received a purse of $500. The 2005 first prize was $1.17million. The trophy is named the Wanamaker trophy after its donor Rodman Wanamaker. The event was designed specifically for professionals and is restricted to them. 20 places out of 156 maximum entries are reserved for American club professionals.

The format was originally matchplay which changed to strokeplay in 1958.

The record for the greatest number of wins is held by Walter Hagen (1921,1924,1925,1926,1927) and Jack Nicklaus (1963,1971,1973,1975,1980) with five wins each. Hagen holds the record for the most consecutive wins with four successes.

David Toms won in 2001 with a 72 hole score of 265, the lowest ever aggregate score recorded in a Major. The PGA also produced the lowest aggregate scores in relation to par in a Major, with Tiger Woods and Bob May both recording 18 under par in 2000. Toms' aggregate in 2001 was 15 under.

One of the most notable achievements in the PGA history was that of John Daly (motto "grip it and rip it") in 1991. He was called into the event with 24 hours notice – he was 9th reserve – and drove to Crooked Stick, Indiana. He then won the event leading from start to finish. Since then Daly won The Open in 1995 but otherwise his performances have been somewhat erratic and his personal life very colourful.

OTHER RECORDS

Oldest winner - Julius Boros 1968, 48 years
Youngest winner - Gene Sarazen 1922, 20 years
Greatest winning margin - Paul Runyan beat Sam Snead
by 8 & 7 in 1938

*A man is taking a very long time over his tee shot
and his partner finally loses patience and says,
"What's the problem, what's taking so long?"
The man replies, "My wife is watching me from the
next green."
His partner says, "You're wasting your time.
You can't possibly hit her from here."*

WINNERS OF THE US PGA CHAMPIONSHIP

2006 Tiger Woods (US)
2005 Phil Mickelson (US)
2004 Vijay Singh (Fiji)
2003 Shaun Micheel (US)
2002 Rich Beem (US)
2001 David Toms (US)
2000 Tiger Woods (US)
1999 Tiger Woods (US)
1998 Vijay Singh (Fiji)
1997 Davis Love III (US)
1996 Mark Brooks (US)
1995 Steve Elkington (Aus)
1994 Nick Price (Zim)
1993 Paul Azinger (US)
1992 Nick Price (Zim)
1991 John Daly (US)
1990 Wayne Grady (Aus)
1989 Payne Stewart (US)
1988 Jeff Sluman (US)
1987 Larry Nelson (US)
1986 Bob Tway (US)
1985 Hubert Green (US)
1984 Lee Trevino (US)
1983 Hal Sutton (US)
1982 Ray Floyd (US)
1981 Larry Nelson (US)
1980 Jack Nicklaus (US)

1979 David Graham (Aus)
1978 John Mahaffey (US)
1977 Lanny Wadkins (US)
1976 Dave Stockton (US)
1975 Jack Nicklaus (US)
1974 Lee Trevino (US)
1973 Jack Nicklaus (US)
1972 Gary Player (SA)
1971 Jack Nicklaus (US)
1970 Dave Stockton (US)
1969 Ray Floyd (US)
1968 Julius Boros (US)
1967 Don January (US)
1966 Al Geiberger (US)
1965 Dave Marr (US)
1964 Bobby Nichols (US)
1963 Jack Nicklaus (US)
1962 Gary Player (SA)
1961 Jerry Barber (US)
1960 Jay Herbert (US)
1959 Bob Rosberg (US)
1958 Dow Finsterwald (US)
1957 Lionel Herbert (US)
1956 Jack Burke Jnr (US)
1955 Doug Ford (US)
1954 Chick Harbert (US)
1953 Walter Burkemo (US)

1952 Jim Turnesa (US)	1934 Paul Runyan (US)
1951 Sam Snead (US)	1933 Gene Sarazen (US)
1950 Chandler Harper (US)	1932 Olin Dutra (US)
1949 Sam Snead (US)	1931 Tom Creavy (US)
1948 Ben Hogan (US)	1930 Tommy Armour (US)
1947 Jim Ferrier (Aus)	1929 Leo Diegel (US)
1946 Ben Hogan (US)	1928 Leo Diegel (US)
1945 Byron Nelson (US)	1927 Walter Hagen (US)
1944 Bob Hamilton (US)	1926 Walter Hagen (US)
1943 *Not Held*	1925 Walter Hagen (US)
1942 Sam Snead (US)	1923 Gene Sarazen (US)
1941 Vic Ghezzi (US)	1922 Gene Sarazen (US)
1940 Byron Nelson (US)	1921 Walter Hagen (US)
1939 Henry Picard (US)	1920 Jock Hutchison (US)
1938 Paul Runyan (US)	1919 Jim Barnes (US)
1937 Denny Shute (US)	1917/18 *First World War*
1936 Denny Shute (US)	1916 Jim Barnes (US)
1935 Johnny Revolta (US)	

*A man and his wife are attending prenatal classes
and the teacher says, "Exercise is good for you.
Walking is very beneficial and perhaps you gentlemen
would like to go walking with your partner."
One man raises his arm to ask a question.
"Yes?" says the teacher.
"Is it OK if she carries a golf bag while we walk?"*

INTERNATIONAL MATCHES

All major team events involve American golfers against international opposition. The three most important matches are the Ryder Cup, Walker Cup and the Presidents Cup.

RYDER CUP

The Ryder Cup is played bi-annually between the USA and Great Britain and Europe. From its inception in 1927 to 1973 it was USA v Great Britain, from 1973 to 1977 it was USA v Great Britain and Ireland, and in 1979 the present format of USA v Great Britain and Europe was instituted. The match alternates between America and Europe.

The first Anglo-American competition was played in 1921 at Gleneagles where the British team won 9-3. The Walker Cup, for amateur golfers, had been founded in 1922 and Sam Ryder, a wealthy seed merchant from St Albans (he was the first to sell seeds in the small packets we know today), proposed in 1925 an annual match between British and American professionals. Ryder actually commissioned the trophy in 1926 but it was not ready in time for the match played that year. That match was played at Wentworth with Ted Ray as British captain and Walter Hagen as American captain. Britain won by the massive margin of 13.5 to 1.5 and the likeness now adorning the Ryder Cup is that of Abe Mitchell, a member of the British team. This match was considered to be "unofficial" and some controversy occurred as three of the US team, Tommy Armour, Jim Barnes, and Fred McLeod, were British born. The rules of the new cup stipulated that the players must be native born and the first official Ryder Cup was played in Worcester, Mass, in 1927 and was won by the US 9.5 to 2.5.

Throughout the 1960s the GB team suffered a series of heavy losses, and both the public and the golfers themselves began to lose interest in the event. Irish players were then added to the competition, however the large US winning margins continued and after the 1977 match Jack Nicklaus led the movement to alter the terms of the event and include European players. It took until the 1983 match for the GBE team to mount a serious challenge, losing 14.5 to 13.5, and thereafter the Ryder Cup has become a much more competitive event attracting enormous public interest. Since 1983 GBE has won seven cups against three for the US.

RESULTS

1927	US 9.5	GB 2.5
1929	GB 7.0	US 5.0
1931	US 9.0	GB 3.0
1933	GB 6.5	US 5.5
1935	US 9.0	GB 3.0
1937	US 8.0	GB 4.0
1947	US 11.0	GB 1.0
1949	US 7.0	GB 5.0
1951	US 9.5	GB 2.5
1953	US 6.5	GB 5.5
1955	US 8.0	GB 4.0
1957	GB 7.5	US 4.5
1959	US 8.5	GB 3.5
1961	US 14.5	GB 9.5
1963	US 23.0	GB 9.0

1965	US 19.5	GB 12.5
1967	US 23.5	GB 8.5
1969	US 16.0	GB 16.0
1971	US 18.5	GB 13.5
1973	US 19.0	GBI 13.0
1975	US 21.0	GBI 11.0
1977	US 12.5	GBI 7.5
1979	US 17.0	GBE 11.0
1981	US 18.5	GBE 9.5
1983	US 14.5	GBE 13.5
1985	GBE 16.5	US 11.5
1987	GBE 15.0	US 13.0
1989	GBE 14.0	US 14.0
1991	US 14.5	GBE 13.5
1993	US 15.0	GBE 13.0
1995	GBE 14.5	US 13.5
1997	GBE 14.5	US 13.5
1999	US 14.5	GBE 13.5
2002	GBE 15.5	US 12.5
2004	GBE 18.5	US 9.5
2006	GBE 18.5	US 9.5

Other Ryder Cup Records

Most appearances - Nick Faldo 11
Most matches played - Nick Faldo 46
Youngest player - Sergio Garcia 19
Oldest player - Ray Floyd 51
Most points won - Nick Faldo 25
Most matches won - Nick Faldo 23
Most singles won - Nick Faldo, Peter Oosterhuis,
Arnold Palmer, Billy Casper,
Lee Trevino, Sam Snead. *All with 6 wins.*
Most foursomes won Bernhard Langer 12
Most four ball wins Ian Woosnam 10
Most losing matches - Neil Coles,
Christy O'Connor Snr. 21

As readers will see from the above, most of these records emanate from the period of the 1980s and 1990s, the period of GBE domination of the event. The achievements of Nick Faldo stand out in Ryder Cup history.

WALKER CUP

The Walker Cup commenced in 1922 at Southampton GC, New York. The idea for the event came from a meeting between the R&A and the USGA held at St Andrews in 1920 which discussed rule changes, and the idea of international amateur competitions was raised. The idea was enthusiastically taken up by George Herbert Walker, the USGA President, and in 1921 the USGA invited a number of countries to send teams to compete for what the press had dubbed the "Walker Cup", but no country sent a team that year. However a US team led by William Fownes played against a British team at Hoylake prior to the British Amateur Championship. The Americans won by 9 to 3.

George Walker was the grandfather of George Herbert Bush, former US President, and the great-grandfather of George W (Walker) Bush, the current President.

In 1922 the R&A sent a British team to compete for the Cup. The event was held at Southampton, NY, the home club of George Walker. This first official match was won by the USA 8 to 4. Thereafter the Walker Cup was restricted to USA and Great Britain and Ireland and was held annually until 1924 and bi-annually since that time.

The format is similar to the Ryder Cup with teams of eight players. Currently the US leads the series with 33 wins, 7 losses, and 1 tie. Despite this US domination, European players have not been added to the GBI team, and the results have changed significantly in recent years. GBI has won 4 of the last 6 Walker Cups.

Much of the dominance of the US in the Walker Cup can be attributed to the policy of the USGA to include college golfers on golf scholarships in their teams, whereas the R&A maintains a stricter definition of amateur status. Well known American professionals who have played in the Cup include:-

Gene Littler – Tommy Aaron – Lanny Wadkins
Tom Kite – Scott Simpson – Hal Sutton – Corey Pavin
Davis Love III – Duffy Waldorf – Scott Verplank
Billy Mayfair – Phil Mickelson – Tiger Woods

British players who have gone on to professional success include:-

Sandy Lyle – Colin Montgomerie
Ronan Rafferty – Peter Oosterhuis
Peter Townshend – David Gilford – David Graham

WALKER CUP WINNERS

2005	US 12.5	GBI 11.5
2003	GBI 12.5	US 11.5
2001	GBI 15	US 9
1999	GBI 15	US 9
1997	US 18	GBI 6
1995	GBI 14	US 10

1993	US 19	GBI 5
1991	US 14	GBI 10
1989	GBI 12.5	US 11.5
1987	US 16.5	GBI 7.5
1985	US 13	GBI 11
1983	US 13.5	GBI 10.5
1981	US 15	GBI 9
1979	US 15.5	GBI 8.5
1977	US 16	GBI 8
1975	US 15.5	GBI 8.5
1973	US 14	GBI 10
1971	GBI 13	US 11
1969	US 10	GBI 8
1967	US 13	GBI 7
1965	US 11	GBI 11
1963	US 12	GBI 8
1961	US 11	GBI 1
1959	US 9	GBI 3
1957	US 8.5	GBI 3.5
1955	US 10	GBI 2
1953	US 9	GBI 3
1951	US 7.5	GBI 4.5
1949	US 10	GBI 2
1947	US 8	GBI 4
1938	GBI 7.5	US 4.5
1936	US 10.5	GBI 1.5
1934	US 9.5	GBI 2.5
1932	US 9.5	GBI 2.5
1930	US 10	GBI 2
1928	US 11	GBI 1
1926	US 6.5	GBI 5.5
1924	US 9	GBI 3
1923	US 6.5	GBI 5.5
1922	US 8	GBI 4

PRESIDENTS CUP

The Presidents Cup is played bi-annually by professional golfers between USA and the rest of the world, excluding Europe. It is played in non-Ryder Cup years and the location alternates between USA and the rest of the world. The format is similar to the Ryder Cup with singles, foursomes and fourball matches and a total of twelve players in each team.

PRESIDENTS CUP WINNERS

2005	USA 18.5	ROW 15.5
2003	USA 17	ROW 17
2000	USA 21.5	ROW 10.5
1998	ROW 20.5	USA 11.5
1996	USA 16.5	ROW 15.5
1994	USA 20	ROW 12

The idea for this event came from the US PGA although it is often associated with Bill Clinton who was President of the USA at that time, and is a keen amateur golfer.

Up until 2003 the Presidents Cup had a format whereby, if there was a tie, one player from each side would play a sudden death tiebreaker match. That year the main match ended with a 17-17 tie and Tiger Woods played Ernie Els in the tiebreaker which had to be stopped because of the arrival of darkness. Captains Jack Nicklaus and Gary Player decided that the trophy would be shared. Starting with the 2005 event, the tiebreaker has been scrapped, however all singles matches must be played to a finish, involving extra holes if required.

GREAT GOLFERS

Any listing of golfers is by definition selective. My list involves interesting players of the past, and living players who have finished their main careers. Present day tournament players presumably have more achievements to record, and some future author can document their complete careers. Neither do I intend to get involved in debate as to comparisons between players of different vintages. Whereas I know that modern players are bigger, fitter, and better nourished than their predecessors, and are better equipped, and would most likely defeat these ghosts, there is no method to resolve these theoretical contests and I shall not waste time on them except to say that there is little doubt that Tiger Woods will be the best golfer of all time.

OLD TOM MORRIS

Old Tom was born in St Andrews in 1821. As a teenager he was apprenticed to Allan Robertson who was a local maker of clubs and balls as well as being a fine golfer. During the 1840s the new gutty balls arrived on the scene. Robertson insisted on continuing to make featheries whilst Morris preferred the new gutties which had superior performance, so Morris moved to Prestwick as professional in 1851.

Morris played in the first Open at Prestwick in 1861 which he was expected to win but lost to Willie Park Senior. He subsequently won four Opens.

Old Tom returned to St Andrews as greenkeeper to the R&A in 1866 and remained there until his retirement in 1906. He played in the Open until 1896 aged 75 years. He died in 1908.

Winner:-
The Open: 1861,1862,1864,1867.

·············· YOUNG TOM MORRIS ··············

Young Tom Morris, son of Old Tom, was born in St Andrews in 1851. He was taught by his father at Prestwick, turning professional in 1867 at the age of 16. The next year he won the Open for the first of his four victories. In 1870 he won the Open for the third time and kept the Championship Belt, which was replaced in 1872 by the famous claret jug. Morris scored his fourth consecutive win in 1872 (event not held 1871). His career was shortlived however. His wife died in childbirth in 1875 and Morris never recovered from the shock. He died the same year aged only 24.

Winner:-
The Open: 1868,1869,1870,1872.

················ HARRY VARDON ················

Harry Vardon was one of the "Triumvirate" with J H Taylor and James Braid. This Triumvirate dominated golf from 1894 to 1914. During this period they won sixteen Open Championships. Taylor and Braid, together with Willie Auchterlonie, were the first professionals to be elected members of the R&A in 1950.

Vardon was born in Jersey in 1870 and died in 1937. He started work as a gardener in Jersey but played golf on the course at Grouville. His brother Tom became professional at St Annes, Lancashire, and Harry became assistant professional at Ripon in 1890, becoming professional at Ganton in 1896, in which year he beat J H Taylor, the reigning Open champion, by 8&6. This brought Vardon to the notice of the golfing world and he embarked on his career as a playing professional. The same year, 1896, he beat Taylor in a playoff to win the first of his six Opens.

In 1900 Vardon and Taylor travelled to America and competed in the US Open. Vardon won and Taylor came second. Vardon became ill in 1903 and dropped out of golf events until 1911 when he again won the Open. He returned to America in 1913 where he and Ted Ray lost in a playoff to Francis Ouimet. Vardon won his last Open title in 1914.

The famous "Vardon grip" with the little finger of the right hand overlapping the index finger of the left, was not in fact invented by Vardon, but was used by him, and it is due to him that this is still the standard grip used today.

Winner:-
The Open: 1896,1898,1899,1903,1911,1914.
US Open: 1900
German Open: 1911

J H TAYLOR

John Henry Taylor was born in Devon in 1871 and died in 1963. He started as a caddie at Westward Ho!, later becoming professional there and subsequently at

Burnham-on-Sea. He entered his first Open in 1893, becoming the first non-Scottish professional winner, and won the subsequent two in 1894 and 1895. He won a further three Opens. He lived on to a great age and was well known as a speaker, clubmaker, and course designer. Royal Mid Surrey is one of his courses.

Winner:-
The Open: 1894,1895,1900,1909,1913.
French Open: 1980,1909
German Open: 1912

JAMES BRAID

James Braid was born in Fife in 1870 and died in London in 1950. Although he played golf from an early age, Braid played as an amateur for some years, and worked as a joiner before turning professional. He won his first Open at Muirfield in 1901 at the age of 31, and went on to win four more Opens over the next ten years. He was club professional at Walton Heath from 1904 to his death in 1950.

Winner:-
The Open: 1901,1905,1906,1908,1910
French Open: 1910

WALTER HAGEN

Walter Hagen was born in Rochester, NY, in 1892 and died in 1969. He was arguably the first of the great American professional golfers and the first player to attack the previous dominance of the Scottish and English golfers.

He started out by practicing in a cow pasture with clubs he had made himself, and he continued to play with self-made clubs throughout his career. He became a caddie at the Rochester Country Club whilst working at a variety of jobs, including taxidermy. He first played in the US Open in 1913 at the age of twenty and won his first US Open title the next year. He had in fact wanted to be a baseball player and had trials for the Philadelphia Phillies as a pitcher, however he now became firmly set on a career in golf.

He was a flamboyant dresser and a great party animal. He was a great friend of Al Jolson and their drinking exploits were legendary. Hagen tied for the US Open title in Boston in 1919 and was scheduled to play in the playoff the next day. He partied all night with Jolson but still managed to win the playoff by one shot, having gone to the first tee straight from the party. In 1922 Hagen became the first American-born winner of the Open at Royal St Georges. On the night before the first round, Hagen was still drinking at 2 am and someone reminded him that his opponents were all in bed. Hagen replied, "Maybe they're in bed but they're not sleeping."

Hagen was especially scornful of the snobbery which he, as a professional, encountered in golf. He travelled to England for the first time in 1920 for the Open at Deal. He found that he was not allowed in the clubhouse, so he hired a Daimler limousine which his chauffeur parked in front of the main entrance and changed in it without bothering to be discreet. He also hired a butler who met him on the 18th green each day with a drink on a tray.

In 1918 Hagen was appointed as professional at Oakland Hills, Detroit, where the boom and growth in automobile manufacture was creating new wealth for individuals who were not concerned with the social niceties prevailing in the eastern US. Hagen was an honoured full member of the club and admitted to the clubhouse.

Winner:-
The Open: 1922,1924,1928,1929.
US Open: 1914,1919,
US PGA: 1921,1924,1925,1926,1927.
French Open: 1920
Canadian Open: 1931
Ryder Cup: 1927,1929,1931,1933,1935.

···················GENE SARAZEN···················

Eugenio Saraceno was born in Harrison, NY, in 1902 and died in 1997. He was the first player to win all four majors although for much of his career he was overshadowed by Walter Hagen.

Sarazen is often best remembered for some incredible single shots, most notably "the shot that was heard around the world". This occurred at the 1935 Masters final round on the 15th hole where, after his tee shot, Sarazen had 220 yards remaining to the green. He was three shots behind the leader Craig Wood and had a poor lie. He took some time considering the shot until his playing partner Walter Hagen said, "Hurry it up willya! I've got a date tonight." Sarazen took a four wood and holed the shot for an albatross and tied with Wood after the 72 holes. He easily won the playoff the next day.

Another remarkable shot played by Sarazen was at the 1923 US Open where he was playing Walter Hagen in the final. At the second extra hole Sarazen had hit into the woods and his ball had bounced off the roof of a hut and remained in bounds. Sarazen hit his shot through the trees to within three feet of the hole and Hagen was so shaken that he missed an easy putt and the championship. The last unique shot was at the 1973 Open at Troon where Sarazen, at the age of 71, holed in one. In 1997, one month before his death at the age of 97, he drove off the Masters.

Sarazen's lasting gift to golf is the invention of the sand iron.

Winner:-
The Open: 1932
US Open: 1922,1932
US PGA: 1922,1923,1933
US Masters: 1935
Ryder Cup: 1927,1929, 1931,1933,1935,1937,1939

BOBBY JONES

Unlike the majority of professional golfers of his era, Bobby Jones was born into a family of some wealth and remained an amateur all his life. He was born in Atlanta in 1902 and died there in 1971. Bobby was a sickly child and his father introduced him to golf in an effort to improve his health. He graduated in engineering at Georgia Tech before studying at Harvard. He eventually qualified in law and had his own practice.

Jones played from the age of seven at East Lake, Atlanta, where the family had a house next to the course. He was taught by a Scots professional, Stewart Maiden, who

remained his mentor throughout his career. Jones won the
Georgia State Amateur aged fourteen and at fifteen won
the Southern Amateur Championship. At seventeen he
was runner-up in the US Amateur Championship and the
Canadian Open.

From age fifteen to twenty-two, Jones suffered the "seven
lean years", a phrase coined by Atlanta journalist O B
Keeler, who closely followed Jones's career. Part of his
problem was his fiery temper which he eventually learned
to control. At the 1921 Open at St Andrews, he picked up
his ball and walked off the course. This phase terminated
at the US Open in 1923 where Jones beat Bobby
Cruikshank in a playoff, after surrendering a four shot
lead over the final four holes of normal play.

Between 1923 and 1930 Jones won thirteen national
championships culminating in 1930 when he won the
British and US Opens and the British and US Amateur
Championships. That same year he retired from competitive events at the age of 28. He carried on as a fine
teacher of the game and was a prolific writer. His widely
syndicated weekly newspaper columns were full of shrewd
advice for golfers. Perhaps the most well-known and
succinct is "Nobody ever swung a golf club too slowly."

Jones continued to play in casual and exhibition matches
until he became paralysed by an acute spinal condition at
the age of 48 and was confined to a wheelchair. He was
made a freeman of St Andrews in 1958 and the USGA
instituted the Bob Jones Award, which is its highest
honour, for distinguished achievements in golf. Many still
regard him as the greatest golfer of all time.

Winner:-
The Open: 1923,1926,1929
US Open: 1923,1926,1929,1930
US Amateur: 1924,1925,1927,1928,1930
British Amateur: 1930
Walker Cup: 1922,1924,1926,1928,1930

"Competitive golf is played mainly on a five and a half inch course, the space between your ears."
Bobby Jones.

····················· # BYRON NELSON ·····················

Byron Nelson was born in Fort Worth, Texas, in 1912 and died in 1997. After initially struggling as a professional, he worked hard and patiently on his technique and was rewarded in 1937 when he won the Masters. One of his maxims was "It is next to impossible to stand too close to the ball." He is reputed to have had the most perfect and relaxed swing of all time, and the USGA machine which tested the properties of golf balls was known as "Iron Byron".

Nelson is most famous for what became known as "The Streak". In 1945, he won 19 out of 34 tournaments he entered and was second in seven of them. He won eleven of these events in a row. His average round over all these tournaments was 68.33. To this day the next longest winning sequence is four, by Jack Burke in 1952.

One year after The Streak in 1946, Nelson largely retired from competitive golf although he did win the French Open in 1955 whilst on holiday there.

Winner:-
US Open: 1939
Masters: 1937,1942
US PGA: 1940,1945
French Open: 1955
Ryder Cup: 1937,1939,1947

> *"The only shots you can be dead sure of*
> *are those you've had already."*
> Byron Nelson.

···················· SAM SNEAD ····················

Sam Snead was born in Virginia in 1912 and died in 2002. Like many of the American professionals he came from an impoverished background, and later in his career became known as "the affluent hillbilly".

Snead was self-taught and started playing with home-made clubs. He joined the professional circuit in 1933 and began winning tournaments almost immediately. He still today holds the record for the most tournament wins with 84 successes.

It took longer for Snead to progress to winning Majors, the first being the US PGA in 1942. Undoubtedly his career was affected by the war, however it was after the war that his best results occurred. Between 1946 and 1954 he won three of the Majors but was never able to win the US Open. He went on to be one of the best ever senior players, and he won the Seniors PGA six times.

In 1960, Snead was granted an audience with the Pope,

and brought his putter along to be blessed. One of the cardinals remarked "My putting is hopeless too" to which Snead replied "If you live here and can't putt, what chance is there for me?"

Discussion still takes place today as to whether Snead or his contemporary Byron Nelson had the best swing.

Winner:-
The Open: 1946
Masters: 1949,1952,1954
US PGA: 1942,1949,1951
Canadian Open: 1938,1940,1941
Ryder Cup: 1937,1939,1947,1949,1951,1953,1955, 1959
Seniors PGA: 1964,1965,1967,1970,1972,1973

BEN HOGAN

Born in Dublin, Texas, in 1912, the same year as Snead and Nelson, Ben Hogan began as a caddie in Fort Worth, Texas. In 1930 he tied with Byron Nelson for the local caddies championship. He became professional in 1931, but was not initially successful. This is often attributed to the fact that he was naturally left-handed but was forced to play right-handed by the lack of left-handed clubs at that time.

His first Major win was the US PGA in 1946 he went on to win the PGA and the US Open in 1948. He was then involved in a horrific car crash in 1949 which almost killed him, and it was presumed that he would never play golf again. However Hogan was determined to play again, and tied with Sam Snead at the LA Open in 1950. He followed this by winning the US Open in 1950 and 1951.

In 1953 Hogan won all six tournaments he entered including the British and US Opens and the Masters. He did not play in the PGA because the dates clashed with the British Open. This was the only occasion he played in the British Open. He was known in Scotland as the "Wee Ice Man" and in America as "The Hawk".

Hogan is generally regarded as the best shot maker of all time, but he was often let down by his putting. He died in Texas in 1997.

Winner:-
The Open: 1953
US Open: 1948,1950,1951,1953
Masters: 1951,1953
US PGA: 1946,1948
Ryder Cup: 1941,1947,1951

SIR HENRY COTTON

Henry Cotton was born in Cheshire in 1907 and died in Portugal in 1987. He won the Open at Sandwich in 1934 ending 11 years of American domination. His round of 65 held the record for the Open until 1977. The Dunlop 65 golf ball was named after this round. Cotton is considered by many to be the greatest British golfer.

His career was severely truncated by the war but he came back to win the Open in 1948.

At age 50, Cotton retired to Penina, Portugal, where he designed and ran the golf course. He was posthumously knighted following his death in 1987.

Winner:-
The Open: 1934,1937,1948
Ryder Cup: 1929,1937,1947
Belgian Open: 1930,1934,1938
Italian Open: 1936
French Open: 1946,1947
German Open: 1937,1938,1939

BOBBY LOCKE

Arthur D'Arcy Locke was born in South Africa in 1917. He was the leading amateur in the 1936 British Open after which he turned professional. His career was severely affected by the war which he spent as a bomber pilot.

He returned after the war and at first played in South Africa, where he won a series of games against Sam Snead.

He played in America in 1946 to 1947 and won six events and came second in two others. He was second to Jimmy Demaret in the money winners' list. In 1948 he won the Chicago Victory National by 16 strokes which still stands today as the biggest ever winning margin on the PGA Tour. His first Major success was the British Open in 1949 after which he was barred from the US circuit for a

time due to a dispute about playing commitments. The
ban was lifted in 1951 but Locke never again played in
America. He went on to win three more British Opens. A
car crash in 1959 impaired his sight and finished his playing career. He died in 1987.

Locke played with a unique technique and he was no
stylist. Off the tee he was not a long hitter and hit every
shot with a pronounced hook but they nearly always
landed on the fairway. His putting however was superb,
even though his technique on the greens was as bizarre as
on the tees. Many will say that he was the best putter of
all time.

Winner:-
The Open: 1949,1950,1952,1957
South African Open: 1935,1937,1938,1939,1940,1946,
    1950,1951,1955
Irish Open: 1938
NZ Open: 1938
Canadian Open: 1947
French Open: 1952,1953

PETER THOMSON

Peter Thomson was born in Melbourne, Australia, in
1929. His great achievement in golf was a total of five
wins in the Open, still the record. He not only won five
times but from 1952 to 1958 he always finished in the top
two. His hat-trick of three wins 1954-56 also remains
unequalled since 1882.

Thomson's reputation was diminished by the fact that he
did not perform well on the US circuit. His best result in
America was winning the Texas Open in 1956. He never

finished higher than fourth in any of the US Majors. This
negative performance in the US was transformed later in
Thomson's career when he played on the Seniors Tour in
the 1980s. He won nine events in 1985 and was the
leading money winner.

Thomson was not only a golfer. He was involved in
Australian politics at one time and is a well known journalist and artist.

Winner:-
The Open: 1954,1955,1956,1958,1965
British Matchplay: 1954,1961,1966,1967
Australian Open: 1951,1967

·················ARNOLD PALMER·················

Arnold Palmer was born in Pennsylvania in 1929. His
father was the professional at the Latrobe Country Club
and Arnold played golf from an early age. He became the
US Amateur champion in 1954 and turned professional
immediately after. He won his first professional tournament, the Canadian Open, the next year and his first
Major, the Masters, in 1958. In 1960 he won the Masters
again followed by the US Open which he won by over-
coming a seven shot deficit on the final day. Also in 1960
he played his first British Open where he came second to
Kel Nagle. He won the next two Opens in 1961 and
1962.

Palmer was not noted for his playing style, but what he
may have lacked in finesse he made up for in strength and
determination. He is quoted as saying "Take the club
back smoothly, make a big turn, start down smoothly with
the hips, then hit it hard."

Palmer could be erratic on the course. He once hit four successive tee shots into the sea in Los Angeles, and he lost the 1966 US Open to Billy Casper giving up a seven shot lead with nine holes to play.

Most importantly, Palmer was the first golfer of the television era. He was widely admired, building up a large fan base known as "Arnie's Army", and was a great ambassador for the game of golf. In 1960 he was voted "Sportsman of the Year" by Sports Illustrated He gets much of the credit for the huge rise in the popularity of golf in the modern era. He is the first ever million dollar winner in golf.

He competed in the Masters for the last time in 2004, his 50th consecutive appearance in the event.

As well as playing golf, Palmer built up major business interests including ownership of the Bay Hill course and of the Latrobe Country Club where his father had been the professional, and where young Arnie was only allowed to play in the early morning or late evening when the members weren't playing. There is also a drink called an "Arnold Palmer" which is a mixture of iced tea and lemonade. This drink is popular at US golf clubs but so far has not managed to overtake beer as the main drink in British clubs. I wonder why?

Winner:-
The Open: 1961,1962
US Open: 1960
US Masters: 1958,1960,1962,1964
World Matchplay: 1964,1967
Ryder Cup: 1961,1963,1965,1967,1971,1973

Arnold Palmer is playing golf with Tiger Woods and on the 10th hole Tiger's tee shot lands right behind a fifty foot tree. Tiger says to Arnie "How would you play this one – take a drop?" Arnie replies "When I was your age I played right over the tree." Tiger plays the shot which hits the branches and goes out of bounds. Tiger asks Arnie "How did you ever play that shot?" Arnie replies "When I was your age that tree was only two feet high."

Arnold Palmer is playing a round with Jesus and Jesus shanks his shot which lands on an island in the middle of a lake. Jesus walks across the water to take his shot and Arnie says "Jesus, who do you think you are? Jack Nicklaus?"

GARY PLAYER

Gary Player was born in Johannesburg in 1935. He was already a professional golfer when he arrived in Britain in 1954 and his first success was the Dunlop Masters in 1956. Player is quite a small man and he had some difficulty competing for distance with other professionals. He compensated for this by undertaking a fitness and body-building regime, something which is common with golf professionals today, but was almost unheard of in the 1950s.

Thus fortified, Player won the British Open in 1959, the Masters in 1961, and the US PGA in 1962. He became one of the big three consisting of himself, Palmer, and Nicklaus. He was an especially fine matchplay exponent winning the World Matchplay event five times. Until quite recently he competed successfully on the Seniors circuit both in USA and Britain.

Winner:-
The Open: 1959,1968,1974
US Open: 1965
US Masters: 1961,1974,1978
US PGA: 1962,1972
World Matchplay: 1965,1966,1968,1971,1973
Australian Open: 7 times
South African Open: 13 times.

> *"The more I practice, the luckier I get."*
> Gary Player.

JACK NICKLAUS

Jack Nicklaus was born in Columbus, Ohio, in 1940. He suffered from polio as a child, but made a full recovery and started playing golf at the age of ten. His golf career started when his father injured his ankle and was advised to walk a few miles each day as therapy, so he took up golf with young Jack as his caddie. During his high school days Nicklaus won six consecutive Ohio junior titles, the first one at the age of twelve. He went to Ohio State University in 1958 and whilst there he won the US Amateur title twice in 1959 and 1961. He also came second in the US Open in 1960, losing by two shots to Arnold Palmer. After a short period as an apprentice pharmacist, his father's profession, Nicklaus turned professional in 1962.

Nicklaus was quickly into his stride and won the US Open in his first season and the Masters and the US PGA in the following year, 1963. The Nicklaus – Palmer rivalry during the 1960s (joined by Gary Player) was a major element in the increasing popularity of golf both as a spectator and participant sport. These three came to be known as "The Modern Triumvirate" and dominated the game of golf during the 1960s.

Nicklaus went on to become the golfer with the best record of all time. He won 18 Majors and was second 19 times. He won 73 PGA tournaments in his career, second to Sam Snead. He topped the PGA money winner's list eight times. He is one of only five players to have won all four grand slam events during his career and is the only golfer to have won all four events at least three times. Later in his career he won ten events on the Senior PGA tour.

In 2005 The Royal Bank of Scotland issued banknotes incorporating Nicklaus's picture. This is the only recorded occurrence of a golfer appearing on a monetary instrument.

Of all golfers, Nicklaus is probably the one who has achieved the greatest commercial success. His "Golden Bear" range of golf equipment and clothing is sold world-wide and his company Golden Bear Inc designs, builds, and manages golf courses all over the world. Its annual turnover exceeds $120 million.

Perhaps most of all, Nicklaus is famed for his quiet temperament and demeanor and for his pleasant manner.

Winner:-
The Open: 1966,1970,1978
US Open: 1962,1967,1972,1980
US Masters: 1963,1965,1966,1972,1975,1986
US PGA: 1963,1971,1973,1975,1980

Australian Open: 1964,1968,1971,1975,1976,1978
Ryder Cup: 1969,1971,1973,1975,1977,1981

> *"I think I fail just a bit less then everyone else."*
> Jack Nicklaus

> *"Jack Nicklaus plays a game with which*
> *I am not familiar."*
> Bobby Jones

> *"Jack Nicklaus has become a legend in his own spare time."*
> Gene Sarazen

···················TOM WATSON···················

Tom Watson was born in Kansas City, Missouri, in 1949. He started golf at an early age and was a fine junior player. He graduated in psychology from Stanford in 1971, but immediately started as a golf professional.

Watson's first Major win was the British Open in 1975 and he went on to win this event five times over an eight year period. This compares with a total of three Major wins in the USA, one Open and two Masters. Watson is still held in great esteem in Britain and in 1999 he was elected to honorary membership of the R&A. He was named PGA Player of the Year six times, being second in this category behind Tiger Woods who has already held that title seven times.

Watson had a number of memorable battles with Jack Nicklaus. The most famous was at the US Open at Pebble Beach in 1982. Nicklaus was in the clubhouse being interviewed on TV as the likely winner, when Watson shot out of the rough on the 17th, hit the flagstick, and the ball fell into the hole. Watson then birdied the 18th to win by two shots.

Most of all, Watson is known as a friendly, likeable and approachable man. In 1987 he received the Bob Jones Award from the USGA in recognition of his distinguished sportsmanship. He had a long working arrangement with his caddie Bruce Edwards and was visibly very upset when Edwards died from Lou Gehrigs disease in 2004. He is also a principled man – he resigned from his lifetime home club, Kansas City Country Club, due to its policy of not admitting Jewish members.

Winner:-
The Open: 1975,1977,1980,1982,1983
US Open: 1982
US Masters: 1977,1981
Ryder Cup: 1977,1981,1983,1989

"Caddy, stop checking your watch all the time."
"This isn't a watch, sir, it's a compass."

Three members of a fourball game are having a furious argument on the 18th green whilst the fourth member is lying dead on the fairway. The club captain is called to sort things out, and asks what the problem is. "Well," says one of the players, "my partner Jack has had a stroke and these two want to add it to my score."

LADIES GOLF

As mentioned earlier in this book, Mary Queen of Scots is recorded as playing golf in the mid 16th century, so it is therefore clear that ladies, at least aristocratic ones, have played golf since its early stages. It is however equally clear that throughout the last 450 years, ladies have played golf in an often hostile atmosphere, and have suffered enormous prejudice and problems. This continues even today although it is becoming less frequent. Joyce Wethered recalled waiting in the car park for her male golfing partners, as she was not permitted to enter the clubhouse, and keeping her hands warm on the radiator of her Rolls Royce. The 1984 Curtis Cup was played at Muirfield where the competitors were not allowed to enter the clubhouse. Eventually the ladies were given a short guided tour and a notice was put on the board apologizing to the members for the inconvenience caused by this. There is also the story of the Richmond Golf Club where the secretary refused to allow Queen Mary to enter the clubhouse.

Nevertheless ladies golf has progressed into the modern era with many more women playing the game and professional events of a high standard attracting media interest, sponsorship, and large crowds. Americans have generally tended to dominate the women's game although especially in more recent times, as with the men's game, the rest of the world has made considerable progress. In addition to Britain and the United States, Australia,

Sweden and South Korea are countries who have produced numbers of excellent lady golfers.

Here follows a list of the major ladies tournaments and international competitions.

########## WOMEN'S BRITISH OPEN ##########

The Women's British Open (now sponsored by Weetabix) was instituted by the Ladies Golf Union in 1976. Prior to that date the only national championship was the British Ladies Amateur Championship. The Open became part of the US LPGA tour in 1994. Two players, Karrie Webb and Sherri Steinhauer, have won three titles and one player, Debbie Massey has had two wins. Steinhauer and Massey are the only players to have won in consecutive years.

WINNERS OF THE (WEETABIX) WOMENS BRITISH OPEN.

2006 Sherri Steinhauer (USA)	1997 Karrie Webb (Aus)
2005 Jeong Jang (Kor)	1996 Emilee Klein (USA)
2004 Karen Stupples (Eng)	1995 Karrie Webb (Aus)
2003 Annika Sorenstam (Swe)	1994 Liselotte Neuman (Swe)
2002 Karrie Webb (Aus)	1993 Karen Lunn (Aus)
2001 Se Ri Pak (Kor)	1992 Patty Sheehan (USA)
2000 Sophie Gustafson (Swe)	1991 Penny Grice-Whittaker
1999 Sherri Steinhauer (USA)	(Eng)
1998 Sherri Steinhauer (USA)	1990 Helen Alfredsson (Swe)

1989 Jane Geddes (US)	1981 Debbie Massey (US)
1988 Corrinne Dibnah (Aus)	1980 Debbie Massey (US)
1987 Alison Nicholas (Eng)	1979 Alison Sheard (SA)
1986 Laura Davies (Eng)	1978 Janet Melville (Eng)
1985 Betsy King (US)	1977 Vivien Saunders (Eng)
1984 Ayako Okamoto (Jap)	1976 Jenny Lee Smith (Eng)
1983 *No Tournament*	
1982 Marta Figueras-Dotti (Sp)	

BRITISH LADIES AMATEUR CHAMPIONSHIP

The British Ladies Amateur was inaugurated by the LGU in 1893. Since its inception it has remained as a match-play event, the only major event for men or women to do so.

WINNERS OF THE BRITISH LADIES AMATEUR CHAMPIONSHIP

2006 Belen Mozo	1999 Marine Monnet
2005 Louise Stahle	1998 Kim Rostron
2004 Louise Stahle	1997 Alison Rose
2003 Elisa Serramina	1996 Kelli Kuehne
2002 Rebecca Hudson	1995 Julie Wade Hall
2001 Marta Prieto	1994 Emma Duggleby
2000 Rebecca Hudson	1993 Catriona Lambert

1992 Bemille Pedersen	1965 Brigitte Varangot
1991 Valerie Michaud	1964 Carol Sorenson
1990 Julie Wade Hall	1963 Brigitte Varangot
1989 Helen Dobson	1962 Marley Spearman
1988 Joanne Furby	1961 Marley Spearman
1987 Janet Collingham	1960 Barbara McIntire
1986 Mamie McGuire	1959 Elizabeth Price
1985 Lillian Behan	1958 Jessie Valentine
1984 Jody Rosenthal	1957 Philomena Garvey
1983 Jill Thornhill	1956 Wiffi Smith
1982 Kitrina Douglas	1955 Jessie Valentine
1981 Belle Robertson	1954 Frances Stephens
1980 Anne Quast Sander	1953 Marlene Stewart
1979 Maureen Madill	1952 Moira Paterson
1978 Edwina Kennedy	1951 Catherine MacCann
1977 Angel Uzielli	1950 Lally de St Saveur
1976 Cathy Panton	1949 Frances Stephens
1975 Nancy Roth Syms	1948 Louise Suggs
1974 Carol Semple	1947 Babe Zaharias
1973 Ann Irvin	1946 Jean Hetherington
1972 Michelle Walker	1940/45 Not held
1971 Michelle Walker	1939 Pam Barton
1970 Dinah Oxley	1938 Helen Holm
1969 Catherine Lacoste	1937 Jessie Anderson
1968 Brigitte Varangot	1936 Pam Barton
1967 Elizabeth Chadwick	1935 Wanda Morgan
1966 Elizabeth Chadwick	1934 Helen Holm

1933 Enid Wilson

1932 Enid Wilson

1931 Enid Wilson

1930 Diana Fishwick

1929 Joyce Wethered

1928 Nanette le Blan

1927 Simone de la Chaume

1926 Cecil Leitch

1925 Joyce Wethered

1924 Joyce Wethered

1923 Doris Chambers

1922 Joyce Wethered

1921 Cecil Leitch

1920 Cecil Leitch

1915/19 Not held

1914 Cecil Leitch

1913 Muriel Dodd

1912 Gladys Ravenscroft

1911 Dorothy Campbell

1910 Elsie Grant-Suttie

1909 Dorothy Campbell

1908 Maud Titterton

1907 May Hezlet

1906 W Kennion

1905 Bertha Thompson

1904 Lottie Dodd

1903 Rhona Adair

1902 May Hezlet

1901 Mary Graham

1900 Rhona Adair

1899 May Hezlet

1898 Lena Thomson

1897 Edith Orr

1896 Amy Pascoe

1895 Lady Margaret Scott

1894 Lady Margaret Scott

1893 Lady Margaret Scott

UNITED STATES WOMEN'S OPEN
CHAMPIONSHIP

The US Women's Open was founded by the US LPGA in 1950 and is the oldest major professional ladies tournament.

WINNERS OF THE US WOMEN'S OPEN CHAMPIONSHIP

2006 Annika Sorenstam (Swe)	1987 Laura Davies (Eng)
2005 Birdie Kim (Kor)	1986 Jane Geddes (USA)
2004 Meg Mallon (USA)	1985 Kathy Baker (USA)
2003 Hilary Lunke (USA)	1984 Hollis Stacey (USA)
2002 Juli Inkster (USA)	1983 Jan Stephenson (Aus)
2001 Karrie Webb (Aus)	1982 Janet Anderson (USA)
2000 Karrie Webb (Aus)	1981 Pat Bradley (USA)
1999 Juli Inkster (USA)	1980 Amy Alcott (USA)
1998 Se Ri Pak (Kor)	1979 Jerilyn Britz (USA)
1997 Alison Nicholas (Eng)	1978 Hollis Stacey (USA)
1996 Annika Sorenstam (Swe)	1977 Hollis Stacey (USA)
1995 Annika Sorenstam (Swe)	1976 JoAnne Carner (USA)
1994 Patty Sheehan (USA)	1975 Sandra Palmer (USA)
1993 Lauri Merten (USA)	1974 Sandra Haynie (USA)
1992 Patty Sheehan (USA)	1973 Susie Berning (USA)
1991 Meg Mallon (USA)	1972 Susie Berning (USA)
1990 Betsy King (USA)	1971 JoAnne Carner (USA)
1989 Betsy King (USA)	1970 Donna Caponi (USA)
1988 Liselotte Neumann (Swe)	1969 Donna Caponi (USA)

1968 Susie Berning (USA)	1957 Betsy Rawls (USA)
1967 Catherine Lacoste (am) (Fra)	1956 Kathy Cornelius (USA)
	1955 Fay Crocker (Uruguay)
1966 Sandra Spuzich (USA)	1954 Babe Zaharias (USA)
1965 Carol Mann (USA)	1953 Betsy Rawls (USA)
1964 Mickey Wright (USA)	1952 Louise Suggs (USA)
1963 Mary Mills (USA)	1951 Betsy Rawls (USA)
1962 Murle Lindstrom (USA)	1950 Babe Zaharias (USA)
1961 Mickey Wright (USA)	1949 Louise Suggs (USA)
1960 Betsy Rawls (USA)	1948 Babe Zaharias (USA)
1959 Mickey Wright (USA)	1947 Betty Jameson (USA)
1958 Mickey Wright (USA)	1946 Patty Berg (USA)

UNITED STATES WOMEN'S AMATEUR CHAMPIONSHIP

The US Women's Amateur Championship was established by the USGA in 1895, the same year as the Men's Amateur and the Men's US Open. The winner receives the Robert Cox Cup, first presented in 1896 by Robert Cox who was a British Member of Parliament. In the final event the first two rounds are strokeplay and the top 64 players then play knockout matchplay.

Glenna Collett Vare won this event six times. Other notable winners who progressed into the professional ranks include Babe Zaharias, Patty Berg, Louise Suggs, and Beth Daniel.

WINNERS OF THE US WOMEN'S AMATEUR CHAMPIONSHIP.

2006 Kimberly Kim (USA)

2005 Morgan Pressel (USA)

2004 Jane Park (USA)

2003 Virada
     Nirapathpongporn (USA)

2002 Becky Lucidi (USA)

2001 Meredith Duncan (USA)

2000 Marcy Newton (USA)

1999 Dorothy Delasin (USA)

1998 Grace Park (Kor)

1997 Silvia Cavalleri (Ita)

1996 Kelli Kuehne (USA)

1995 Kelli Kuehne (USA)

1994 Wendy Ward (USA)

1993 Jill McGill (USA)

1992 Vicki Goetze (USA)

1991 Amy Fruhwirth (USA)

1990 Pat Hurst (USA)

1989 Vicki Goetze (USA)

1988 Pearl Sinn (USA)

1987 Kay Cockerill (USA)

1986 Kay Cockerill (USA)

1985 Michiko Hattori (Jap)

1984 Deb Richard (USA)

1983 Joanne Pacillo (USA)

1982 Juli Inkster (USA)

1981 Juli Inkster (USA)

1980 Juli Inkster (USA)

1979 Carolyn Hill (USA)

1978 Cathy Sherk (Can)

1977 Beth Daniel (USA)

1976 Donna Horton (USA)

1975 Beth Daniel (USA)

1974 Cynthia Hill (USA)

1973 Carol Semple (USA)

1972 Mary Budke (USA)

1971 Laura Baugh (USA)

1970 Martha Wilkinson (USA)

1969 Catherine Lacoste (Fra)

1968 JoAnne Gunderson-
     Carner (USA)

1967 Mary Lou Dill (USA)

1966 JoAnne Gunderson-
     Carner (USA)

1965 Jean Ashley (USA)

1964 Barbara McIntire (USA)

1963 Anne Quast (USA)

1962 JoAnne Gunderson (USA)

1961 Anne Quast (USA)

1960 JoAnne Gunderson (USA)

1959 Barbara McIntire (USA)

1958 Anne Quast (USA)

1957 JoAnne Gunderson (USA)

1956 Marlene Stewart (Can)

1955 Patricia Lesser (USA)
1954 Barbara Romack (USA)
1953 Mary Lena Faulk (USA)
1952 Jacqueline Pung (USA)
1951 Dorothy Kirby (USA)
1950 Beverley Hanson (USA)
1949 Dorothy Germain Parker (USA)
1948 Grace Linczyk (USA)
1947 Louise Suggs (USA)
1946 Babe Zaharias (USA)
1940/45 *Not held*
1941 Elizabeth Hicks (USA)
1940 Betty Jameson (USA)
1939 Betty Jameson (USA)
1938 Patty Berg (USA)
1937 Estelle Lawson Page (USA)
1936 Pamela Barton (Eng)
1935 Glenna Collett Vare (USA)
1934 Virginia Van Wie (USA)
1933 Virginia Van Wie (USA)
1932 Virginia Van Wie (USA)
1931 Helen Hicks (USA)
1930 Glenna Collett Vare (USA)
1929 Glenna Collett Vare (USA)
1928 Glenna Collett Vare (USA)
1927 Miriam Burns Horn (USA)
1926 Helen Stetson (USA)
1925 Glenna Collett Vare (USA)
1924 Dorothy Campbell-Hurd (Sco)

1923 Edith Cummings (USA)
1922 Glenna Collett Vare (USA)
1921 Marion Hollins (USA)
1920 Alexa Stirling (USA)
1919 Alexa Stirling (USA)
1917/18 *Not held*
1916 Alexa Stirling (USA)
1915 Florence Vanderbeck (USA)
1914 Kate Harley-Jackson (USA)
1913 Gladys Ravenscroft (USA)
1912 Margaret Curtis (USA)
1911 Margaret Curtis (USA)
1910 Dorothy Campbell (Sco)
1909 Dorothy Campbell (Sco)
1908 Kate Harley (USA)
1907 Margaret Curtis (USA)
1906 Harriott Curtis (USA)
1905 Pauline MacKay (USA)
1904 Georgianna Bishop (USA)
1903 Bessie Anthony (USA)
1902 Genevieve Hecker (USA)
1901 Genevieve Hecker (USA)
1900 Frances Griscom (USA)
1899 Ruth Underhill (USA)
1898 Beatrix Hoyt (USA)
1897 Beatrix Hoyt (USA)
1896 Beatrix Hoyt (USA)
1895 C S Brown (USA)

·················· SOLHEIM CUP ··················

The Solheim Cup commenced in 1990 and is played between teams of professional lady golfers representing USA and Europe. The cup is named after Karsten Solheim, founder of the Ping company, and his wife Louise. Solheim was a keen advocate of a women's competition similar to the Ryder Cup and was personally instrumental in the creation of this event. The format is similar to the Ryder Cup. It is played bi-annually alternating between a European and an American location. USA has performed best so far in this event with six wins to Europe's three.

SOLHEIM CUP RESULTS

2005	USA 15.5	Europe 12.5
2003	Europe 17.5	USA 10.5
2002	USA 15.5	Europe 12.5
2000	Europe 14.5	USA 11.5
1998	USA 16	Europe 12
1996	USA 17	Europe 11
1994	USA 13	Europe 7
1992	Europe 11.5	USA 6.5
1990	USA 11.5	Europe 4.5

·················· CURTIS CUP ··················

The Curtis Cup was first played at Wentworth in 1932 and since that time has been a bi-annual event. It was a long time in its gestation as the first informal match was played in England in 1905 between an American team and a British and Irish team. The US team was led by the Curtis sisters, Harriot (US Amateur Champion 1906) and Margaret (US Amateur Champion 1907, 1911 and 1912) and the silver trophy is named after them. The trophy was originally donated in 1927 but it took until 1932 for the USGA and the LGU to reach agreement. It was originally thought that the French Golf Union would participate but this never occurred. Many of the participants have gone on to great success in golf, both professional and amateur. The youngest ever competitor is Michelle Wie from Hawaii who was fourteen when she took part in the 2004 event.

CURTIS CUP RESULTS

2006	USA 11.5	GBI 6.5
2004	USA 10	GBI 8
2002	USA 11	GBI 7
2000	USA 10	GBI 8
1998	USA 10	GBI 8
1996	GBI 11.5	USA 6.5
1994	GBI 9	USA 9
1992	GBI 10	USA 8
1990	USA 14	GBI 4
1988	GBI 11	USA 7
1986	GBI 13	USA 5
1984	USA 9.5	GBI 8.5
1982	USA 14.5	GBI 3.5
1980	USA 13	GBI 5
1978	USA 12	GBI 6
1976	USA 11.5	GBI 6.5
1974	USA 13	GBI 5
1972	USA 10	GBI 8
1970	USA 11.5	GBI 6.5
1968	USA 10.5	GBI 7.5
1966	USA 13	GBI 5
1964	USA 10.5	GBI 7.5
1962	USA 8	GBI 1
1960	USA 6.5	GBI 2.5

1958	GBI 4.5	USA 4.5
1956	USA 5	GBI 4
1954	USA 6	GBI 3
1952	GBI 5	USA 4
1950	USA 7.5	GBI 1.5
1948	USA 6.5	GBI 2.5
1938	USA 5.5	GBI 3.5
1936	USA 4.5	GBI 4.5
1934	USA 6.5	GBI 6.5
1932	USA 5.5	GBI 5.5

GREAT
LADY GOLFERS

As is the case with men golfers, the list of ladies who could be included in this section is a long one. Again I will not include the current crop of excellent lady golfers and I have limited the list to three individuals who, in their different ways, were not only great golfers but were also exceptional ladies in other ways.

·············· JOYCE WETHERED ··············
(LADY HEATHCOAT-AMORY)

Joyce Wethered was born in Surrey in 1901 but was raised mainly in Devon and Scotland. The Wethered family were wealthy and spent much of the summer in Scotland where Joyce and her brother Roger played at Royal Dornoch. Roger Wethered was also a skilled player who tied for the Open in 1921 and lost the playoff. Roger was initially unwilling to play in the playoff because he had arranged to play cricket that day. He was eventually persuaded to play and lost to Jock Hutchinson. He won the Amateur Championship in 1923.

Joyce entered the English Ladies Championship in 1920 at the age of 19 and won it that year and the next four years. In the final she defeated Cecilia Leitch who was the leading female player at that time.

Wethered lost to Leitch in the final of the 1921 British
Ladies Championship but won in the following year
and three times thereafter. She defeated the great
American player Glenna Collett Vare in 1925 and again
in 1929. Wethered had in fact retired from competitive
golf in 1926 but was persuaded out of retirement in
1929 because Collett Vare had entered the Ladies
Championship. She was similarly enticed out of retirement to play in the 1932 Curtis Cup.

The Wethered family lost their fortune in the 1929 Crash
and Joyce went to work in the golf department in
Fortnum and Mason in London. Because of this she lost
her amateur status and in 1935 she toured America earn-
ing the then considerable sum of £4000 in the process.
She was reinstated as an amateur in 1954 when she was
elected President of the Ladies Golf Union.

In 1937 Wethered married Sir John Heathcoat-Amory, a
neighbour in Devon, and finally retired from competitive
golf. She and her husband were renowned gardeners and
their garden at Knightshayes in Devon is still magnificent
today. She received the Royal Horticultural Society
Medal of Honour for her gardening achievements. Lady
Heathcoat-Amory of Tiverton died in Devon in 1997 at
the age of 96.

Wethered became known as the "Queen of Golf". This
was partly due to her aristocratic background, but also to
her calm attitude and stylish play. Bobby Jones said of her
"I have not played golf with anyone, man or woman, who
made me feel so utterly outclassed". Jones had just played
Wethered in a match played in Atlanta on Jones's home
course. Playing on level terms Jones shot a 71, Wethered
a 74, and the American collegiate champion Charlie Yates

76. She also played a match against Gene Sarazen, Horton Smith and Babe Zaharias, defeating Zaharias by ten strokes. Henry Cotton said of her "In my time, no golfer has stood out so far ahead of his or her contemporaries as Lady Heathcoat-Amory."

Winner:-
English Ladies Amateur Championship:
    1920,1921,1922,1923,1924
British Ladies Amateur Championship:
    1922,1924,1925,1929
Curtis Cup: 1932

················ BABE ZAHARIAS ···················

The majority opinion is probably that Joyce Wethered is the greatest ever female golfer, however clearly the most spectacular and interesting was Babe Zaharias.

Zaharias was born Mildred Ella Didriksen in Texas in 1911. (The name later became Didrikson). Her parents were immigrants from Norway.

As a teenager Didrikson was a sporting phenomenon excelling at many sports. She acquired the nickname Babe (after Babe Ruth) when she hit five home runs in one single baseball game. At high school in Beaumont she excelled at athletics, tennis, baseball, basketball, and swimming. In 1930 Didrikson was recruited to play for the Golden Cyclones basketball team in Dallas. This team was sponsored by the Casualty Insurance Company who also gave her a job in the company. The Golden Cyclones won the ladies national championship in 1931 and Didrikson was picked for the All-American team in 1930,1931, and 1932.

At the same time as playing basketball Didriksen became the best female athlete in the United States and probably the world. In the US National Championships in Evanston, Illinois, in 1932, she won six events and broke four world records in one afternoon. These championships were also a team event. The Illinois Women's Athletic Club, who had 23 competitors, came second with 22 points. The Dallas Golden Cyclones, with one competitor, Didrikson, won with 30 points.

At the 1932 Olympics in Los Angeles, Didrikson won three events, javelin, 80 metres hurdles, and high jump, although she was controversially demoted to second place in the high jump because her technique was deemed illegal. She broke Olympic records in all three of these events.

After the 1932 Games, Didriksen became a professional sportswoman and undertook a number of sporting enterprises. She founded and ran a basketball team named Babe Didrikson's All Americans. She also played for a baseball team called the House of David who all, apart from Babe, sported long beards. She also played billiards and appeared in the theatre playing the harmonica. As a result of these activities Didrikson earned very substantial sums, especially when judged against the background of the Depression.

Didrikson started playing golf in 1933 at the age of 22. She practiced very hard and entered her first tournament in 1934. In 1935 she won the Texas Amateur Championship before the USGA declared her professional. She then played in a series of exhibition matches with Gene Sarazen, one against Joyce Wethered who beat her comfortably.

Babe's life changed considerably in 1938 when she
played in a tournament in
Los Angeles against George
Zaharias. Zaharias was a
professional wrestler who
weighed about 300 pounds
and who was known as
"The Crying Greek from
Cripple Creek". They were
married soon after and
George Zaharias quit the
ring and became her
manager.

During the war Babe gave exhibition games to raise
funds for War Bonds and she was reinststed as an
amateur in 1943. After the war Babe entered her best
period as a golfer. During 1946-47 she is reputed to have
won 17 consecutive tournaments including the British
and US Amateur Championships. The number is actually
13 consecutive events – George and Babe conveniently
forgot a loss in the 1947 US Open, however the fact is
that she won 17 out of 18 events during this period.

Babe turned professional again in 1948 and won the first
of her three US Open titles. She was a founder member
of the Ladies PGA and a major attraction on the embry-
onic LPGA tour, and was the first entry into the LPGA
Hall of Fame in 1951.

In 1953 Babe was diagnosed with colonic cancer and
underwent major surgery. She was back playing golf
within four months and won the 1954 US Open plus four
other events. The cancer returned in 1955 and she died

in 1956 at the age of 42. She was a great and early loss to women's golf and to sport in general. She was voted by Associated Press as the greatest female athlete of the 20th century.

Despite her astonishing achievements Babe was a controversial figure during her lifetime and afterwards. She was brash and rude and full of wisecracks. She would enter the locker room before a tournament and ask loudly "OK who's gonna be second?" During her early years of golf she often tried to hit the ball too hard and could be very erratic. After one event where she played badly she was heard to say "I couldn't hit an elephant's ass with a bull fiddle."

The most controversial element of Babe Zaharias was her sexuality. During her early athletics career she was manly in appearance and wore her hair very short. She was often described in the press as being "Amazon", then a code for lesbian, and there were innuendos that she was in fact a man. Her marriage to George Zaharias took away some of the gossip about her until that marriage publicly started to fall apart. George and Babe initially maintained that they enjoyed a normal relationship. However in 1950 Babe began a relationship with Betty Dodd, a young professional golfer. Dodd lived in the house in Florida with George and Babe and was Babe's main nursemaid during her illness. By this time George had ballooned to about 400 pounds. Babe had numerous spats with the press on these issues, most notably with the writer and journalist Paul Gallico who took a particular dislike to her. At one event a female spectator needled her by asking where her whiskers were. Babe replied "I'm sitting on them, sister, same as you."

Today one can visit the Babe Zaharias Museum in Beaumont, Texas, and play on the Babe Zaharias golf course in Tampa, Florida, which she and George owned before her death. There is considerable doubt that Babe could be called the greatest lady golfer but she is certainly the greatest athlete of either sex to have played golf. Today her name is most often heard in the context of female players such as Annika Sorenstam and Michelle Wie competing in men's PGA events. Babe competed in a number of men's PGA tournaments and made the cut in the 1945 Tuscon Open, the last female player to make the cut in a men's PGA event. I wish today's ladies every success, however Babe's record will probably stand a good time longer.

Winner:-
British Ladies Amateur Championship: 1947
US Women's Open Championship: 1948,1950,1954
US Women's Amateur Championship: 1946

MICKEY WRIGHT

Mary Kathryn Wright was born in California in 1935. She was a brilliant junior golfer and won the US Junior Girls' Championship in 1952 and that same year she lost in the final of the US Women's Amateur, and turned professional shortly after. She won a number of LPGA events and in 1958 won the first of four US Women's Opens. All told during her career she won a total of 82 professional tournaments including the four Opens and four LPGA titles. She still holds the record for most wins in the US Open and the LPGA Championship, and is second behind Kathy Whitworth (88 Wins) in terms of overall victories.

Wright's best year was 1963 when she won 13 events. She won the Vare Trophy for the lowest average score in a season five consecutive years (1960-1964), and was leading money winner four consecutive times (1961-1964).

Wright retired from full time golf at an early age in 1969 due to wrist injuries, but continued to play occasionally. She came out of retirement in 1973 to win the prestigious Dinah Shore tournament.

Mickey Wright still lives quietly in California and rarely makes any public appearances.

Winner:-
US Women's Open: 1958,1959,1961,1964
US LPGA: 1958,1960,1961,1963

"Apart from our comparative lack of strength, too many women possess an even greater weakness on the golf course. Women don't hit the ball as hard as they can. Too many women are so concerned that they won't look graceful swinging hard."
Mickey Wright.

TWO FASCINATING COURSES

There are reckoned to be about 32,000 golf courses in the world with about half of these being in North America.

I have chosen to write about just two courses which have unusually interesting histories.

Royal Dornoch in Scotland has some interesting history. Joyce Wethered learned her golf here and, however badly she was treated, her treatment cannot compare with that handed out to Janet Horne two centuries earlier. Janet Horne was a resident of Dornoch and was the last person executed for witchcraft in Britain in 1727. The 9th hole at Dornoch is still called "The Witch" (all the holes on this course have names), and it is adorned by a pond into which Horne was thrown as part of her trial. This was very much a no-win situation for Horne, because it was believed that if the prisoner drowned she could not be a witch, and if she floated she was a witch. Horne's specific piece of witchcraft was that she was turning her daughter into a horse. This was evident because the daughter had deformed hands and feet allegedly similar to a horse. In the face of this overwhelming evidence Horne was burned at the stake in a barrel of tar, close to what is now the golf course. The validity of the verdict was later thrown into considerable doubt as future generations of the Hornes were born with the same deformations of their hands and feet.

The course at St Enedoc in Rock, Cornwall, was much beloved by John Betjeman, the Poet Laureate. He is buried in St Enedoc church which is situated next to the course. The course is well known for having a bunker which is believed to be the world's largest. Based on his times at St Enedoc, Betjeman wrote a poem "Seaside Golf".

How straight it flew, how long it flew,
It cleared the rutty track,
And soaring, disappeared from view
Beyond the bunkers back,
A glorious, sailing, bounding drive
That made me glad I was alive.

And down the fairway, far along
It glowed a lonely white,
I played an iron sure and strong
And clipped it out of sight,
And spite of grassy banks between
I knew I'd find it on the green.

And so I did. It lay content
Two paces from the pin,
A steady putt and then it went
Oh, most securely in.
The very turf rejoiced to see
That quite unprecedented three.

Ah! Seaweed smells from sandy caves
And thyme and mist in whiffs,
In-coming tide, Atlantic waves
Slapping the sunny cliffs,
Lark song and sea sounds in the air
And splendour, splendour everywhere.

Hopefully every golfer, at least occasionally, gets to experience such elation.

GOLF HUMOUR

As there is a wealth of material on golf generally, so the list of golf jokes is almost endless. Here is a selection of some of those which are printable.

CADDIES

All professional players have caddies who are an important part of the game and who provide vital support and advice for the player. At one time, especially before the invention of the golf trolley, caddies were often used by amateur players, however this is now a rarity except in some Asian countries.

Caddies are famous for giving advice and teaching, and here are a few examples.

"Caddy, this is the worst golf course I've ever played on!!"
"This isn't the golf course, sir, we left that an hour ago."

"Caddy, I've never played this badly before."
"I didn't realize you had played before, sir."

"Caddy, do you think my game is improving?"
"Oh yes, sir. You miss the ball much closer than you used to."

"Caddy, how do you like my game?"
"Very good, sir, but personally I prefer golf."

"Caddy, I'd move heaven and earth to break 100 today."
"Try heaven, sir. You've already moved most of the earth."

·············· LADY GOLFERS ··············

Two ladies met on the first tee and the first one asked the other for her handicap. "I'm a scratch golfer," came the reply. "Really!" said the first lady. "Yes," came the reply, "I write down all my good scores and scratch out the bad ones."

A chauvinist golf club eventually admitted lady members after a long resistance. The ladies were generally pleased but after a few months complained to the board about men urinating on the course. After due consideration the board agreed to grant the ladies equal privileges.

Two men are playing a round and in front are two lady players who are rather slow. One of the men walks ahead to speak to the ladies but turns back before he reaches them. "What happened?" says his partner. "You won't believe it but I couldn't speak to them because one of them is my wife and the other is my mistress." The other says, "I'll speak to them." He returns a few minutes later and says, "You won't believe it but..........."

A golfer goes on holiday and visits a golf club to try to get a game with someone. The professional points out Miss Jones who needs a partner, and so they agree to play a round. Miss Jones is a very good player and wins by two holes. The man asks Miss Jones if she would like to play the following day to which she agrees. This time Miss Jones wins by three holes and some mutual attraction has developed, so they arrange to meet for dinner. After the dinner, which has gone very well, the man asks Miss Jones if she would like to spend the night with him and she says she would but she feels she has to tell him that in fact she is a man. The man is outraged. He says, "You have made a complete fool out of me. You played off the red tees."

GOLF: THE FUTURE

Despite its previous associations with racial and social prejudice, golf has a long and proud history. It is one of the oldest sports still being played on a regular basis and provides interest and recreation for millions of people throughout the world. One of the most appealing features of the game is its accessibility to all ages, and with a little good fortune golf can still be played well into old age. Golf also stands out as a game which continues to maintain the highest standards of fair play and honesty in an age where in many other sports these standards are visibly crumbling in the face of commercial exploitation.

We are however now in an era where the structure of golf is changing. More people are playing golf than ever before, but fewer actually belong to golf clubs. In the modern world, due to family and work commitments, many people find it hard to play regularly and justify the cost of an annual subscription which equates to a high cost per round for the irregular user. "Pay and Play" is the expanding area of golf and the sport will have to come to terms with this. This presents a formidable challenge for traditional golf clubs especially in terms of changing their mentality.

The other major issue facing golf is the advance of technology. The regulatory bodies are struggling to drive a middle course between technological advances, and the need to keep the game within the constraints of reasonable expense and the limitations of existing courses. This will be a continuing process.

Of one thing we can all be sure. In years to come a lot of people will still be driving themselves mad trying to get that little white ball into the hole.

Ed Harris.

London, September 2006.